Building Your Personal Brand as a Developer

Standing Out in the Industry Become a well-known expert and grow your career opportunities

THOMPSON CARTER

All rights reserved

No part of this book may be reproduced, distributed, or transmitted in any form or by any means without the prior written permission of the publisher, except in the case of brief quotations embodied in critical reviews and certain other noncommercial uses permitted by right law.

Table of Content

TABLE OF CONTENTS

Introduction

Building Your Personal Brand as a Developer

In today's competitive tech industry, technical skills alone are no longer enough to stand out. With the sheer volume of talented developers in the market, personal branding has become an essential tool for career growth, professional recognition, and opportunity creation. Whether you are a seasoned software engineer, a freelance consultant, or a budding developer, building a strong personal brand is crucial to showcasing your expertise, connecting with others, and expanding your reach within the global developer community.

This book, *Building Your Personal Brand as a Developer: Standing Out in the Industry*, is your comprehensive guide to creating, developing, and scaling your personal brand in the tech industry. Whether you are just starting out or looking to elevate your existing brand, this book will walk you through the key principles, strategies, and techniques to help you grow your presence, influence, and professional opportunities in an increasingly crowded field.

In this book, we will delve deep into the essential aspects of personal branding—from defining your brand and crafting a compelling story to leveraging content creation, social media, and networking. Through clear, actionable advice and real-world examples, you'll learn how to transform your technical expertise into a recognizable personal brand that resonates with employers, clients, and peers alike.

Why Personal Branding Matters for Developers

In the digital age, we are all brands—whether we consciously choose to be or not. In the past, developers may have focused primarily on their technical skills, assuming that would be enough to get hired or land freelance gigs. However, the landscape has changed. Clients and employers today are not only looking for developers who can write clean code but also for individuals who are communicative, engaged with the tech community, and have a well-established online presence. Your personal brand is what helps you stand out in this environment.

Personal branding is not just about being recognized for your technical abilities; it's about creating a reputation that reflects who you are, what you believe in, and how you can contribute to the tech industry. It's about showcasing your expertise in a way that attracts opportunities—whether it's a new project, speaking engagement, or consulting opportunity.

By crafting a strong personal brand, you open doors to higher-paying jobs, collaborations with industry experts, speaking opportunities at global conferences, and a robust network of clients, followers, and advocates. A strong brand can also offer you more control over your career path, giving you the freedom to work on projects that excite you and pursue your passion.

What This Book Will Teach You

In *Building Your Personal Brand as a Developer*, we explore the multifaceted aspects of personal branding and provide you with the tools and knowledge to build a brand that reflects your unique strengths. We will cover:

1. **Defining Your Personal Brand**: You'll learn how to identify your strengths, values, and niche in the developer community. This is the foundation upon which your entire brand will be built.

2. **Building an Online Presence**: In today's digital-first world, an online presence is crucial. This book

will show you how to set up and optimize your profiles on platforms like GitHub, LinkedIn, and Twitter, and help you create content that speaks to your audience.

3. **Content Creation and Thought Leadership**: Whether you are writing blog posts, creating video tutorials, or hosting podcasts, we'll teach you how to create content that establishes you as an authority in your niche. You'll discover how to build a library of valuable, evergreen content that resonates with your audience.

4. **Networking and Community Engagement**: Successful personal branding goes beyond just posting content online. We will guide you on how to engage with the developer community, whether through open-source contributions, attending meetups, or collaborating on projects. Networking will become an integral part of your brand strategy.

5. **Scaling Your Brand Globally**: Building a personal brand isn't just about local recognition. This book will help you scale your personal brand, turning it into an internationally recognized entity. Learn how to partner with other influencers, leverage paid advertising, and expand your brand's reach.

6. **Overcoming Challenges**: Every developer faces challenges while building a personal brand. From imposter syndrome to burnout, we'll cover how to overcome common obstacles and stay motivated on your personal branding journey.

7. **Sustaining Your Brand Over Time**: Personal branding is a marathon, not a sprint. This book will also explore strategies for maintaining and evolving your brand over the long term, ensuring that it remains relevant and valuable as the tech industry changes.

Real-World Examples and Insights

Throughout this book, we'll explore real-world case studies and stories of developers who have successfully built their personal brands. You'll learn from their successes, as well as the challenges they overcame along the way. These examples will give you practical insights and inspiration, as you embark on your own branding journey.

Who This Book Is For

This book is for developers at every stage of their career. Whether you are just starting out and looking to build your first online portfolio, or you are an experienced developer wanting to grow your influence and attract new opportunities, this book provides you with the tools and strategies to succeed.

- **New Developers**: If you are just starting out in your development career, this book will help you build a personal brand that makes you stand out to potential employers and clients, even before you have extensive experience.
- **Freelancers and Consultants**: If you're already freelancing or consulting, you'll learn how to position yourself as an expert in your field, attract new clients, and build a reputation that generates consistent leads.
- **Experienced Developers**: If you're an established developer, this book will guide you on how to take your brand to the next level by expanding your reach globally, becoming a thought leader in your niche, and ensuring your brand stays relevant in an ever-evolving tech landscape.

Your Journey Starts Here

Building a personal brand may seem like a daunting task, but with the right strategy and persistence, it's a journey that can lead to remarkable career growth and opportunities. *Building Your Personal Brand as a Developer* will be your guide to taking your development career to new heights, transforming you from a skilled coder to a recognized thought leader in the tech community.

Let's begin the journey of building a personal brand that will not only set you apart from others in the tech industry but also open up doors for growth, recognition, and long-term success.

CHAPTER 1

INTRODUCTION TO PERSONAL BRANDING

What is Personal Branding and Why Does It Matter for Developers?

Personal branding is the process of establishing and promoting your unique identity as a professional. It involves crafting a narrative around your skills, values, and experiences, and then presenting that narrative consistently across various platforms and interactions. Personal branding is not just about self-promotion—it's about showcasing your expertise, building trust, and connecting with your audience in a meaningful way.

For developers, personal branding is especially important because the tech industry is highly competitive and constantly evolving. With so many developers offering similar services, standing out becomes crucial. By building a strong personal brand, developers can differentiate themselves from the crowd, demonstrate their expertise, and attract more opportunities.

Think of personal branding as the online presence and reputation you cultivate over time. It's how you present yourself to clients, employers, and peers. Your personal brand is a reflection of your skills, character, and the value you provide to the industry. As you continue to contribute to open-source projects, write blog posts, speak at conferences, or create tutorials, your brand grows stronger, positioning you as a go-to expert in your niche.

The Benefits of Building Your Personal Brand as a Developer

Building a personal brand as a developer comes with a range of benefits that can lead to career growth, increased visibility, and greater opportunities. Here are some of the key advantages:

1. **Increased Visibility and Recognition**: A strong personal brand helps you get noticed in a crowded industry. By actively sharing your knowledge, contributing to projects, and engaging with others, you increase your chances of being seen by potential employers, clients, and collaborators. This visibility can help you stay top-of-mind when opportunities arise.

- o **Example**: A developer who writes blog posts about new JavaScript frameworks may gain recognition among other developers who are interested in learning about these tools. This visibility could lead to job offers or invitations to speak at conferences.

2. **Higher Earning Potential**: Developers with strong personal brands can often command higher rates and salaries. As you build your reputation and prove your expertise, you become more attractive to high-paying clients or employers who are willing to pay a premium for your services.

- o **Example**: A developer who has built a reputation in the React community may attract freelance gigs that pay more due to their specialized knowledge. Similarly, top brands might be willing to pay a higher salary to hire someone with a strong personal brand.

3. **Opportunities for Collaboration**: A strong personal brand opens doors for collaboration. Whether you're looking to partner on a project, contribute to open-source, or collaborate with other developers, having an established

presence makes it easier for others to find and work with you.

- o **Example**: A developer with a significant following on GitHub might get invited to join large open-source projects, allowing them to collaborate with skilled developers from around the world.

4. **Job Security and Career Flexibility**: Building a personal brand creates job security, even in a freelance or contract-based career. A strong brand means you have a network of clients, followers, and peers who recognize your value. Even if one opportunity dries up, others will be waiting because of the reputation you've built.

- o **Example**: If you're an independent developer with a well-established online presence and a strong network, you're less likely to experience long gaps between contracts because potential clients will continuously reach out to you.

5. **Personal Growth and Skill Development**: The process of building your personal brand encourages you to grow professionally. You'll continually learn new technologies, refine your

communication skills, and stay on top of trends. Personal branding is an ongoing process that pushes you to remain relevant in a rapidly changing field.

- o **Example**: Writing technical blog posts or creating tutorials forces you to dive deeper into topics you may have learned only on the surface, improving your own understanding and mastery.

How Personal Branding Can Open New Career Opportunities

Personal branding is not just about making yourself known—it's about creating career opportunities that might not have existed otherwise. Here's how personal branding can directly impact your career trajectory:

1. **Attracting Better Job Offers**: When your personal brand is strong, employers or headhunters will be more likely to reach out to you with job opportunities. Having an established online presence can work in your favor by attracting the attention of recruiters who are looking for top talent. Your brand serves as a digital resume that showcases your skills, experience, and value proposition.

- o **Example**: A developer who regularly writes insightful blog posts and shares coding tutorials on YouTube might receive a job offer from a tech company looking for someone with expertise in a niche area like machine learning or blockchain.

2. **Building a Network of Supporters**: Personal branding allows you to build a network of supporters, including fellow developers, potential clients, and even industry leaders. These relationships are invaluable, as they can lead to new business opportunities, collaborations, or even mentorship.

   - o **Example**: By attending developer meetups and engaging on platforms like LinkedIn or Twitter, you can build connections with other developers who might refer you to clients or help you land new projects.

3. **Creating Passive Income Streams**: As you build your brand, you might open opportunities for passive income. You can create and sell online courses, write eBooks, offer paid memberships, or build products that your audience finds valuable. By diversifying your income streams,

you not only enhance your financial stability but also further cement your position as an expert in your field.

- o **Example**: A developer who specializes in mobile app development could create a course on building apps for iOS and Android, which they can sell on platforms like Udemy or Teachable, generating passive income while reinforcing their personal brand.

4. **Attracting Freelance and Consulting Opportunities**:

   If you're a freelancer or consultant, your personal brand can be your best marketing tool. The stronger your personal brand, the more clients will come to you, reducing the need for constant outreach. A strong personal brand makes it easier to command higher rates and work with prestigious clients.

   - o **Example**: A consultant with a strong personal brand in UX design might receive direct inquiries from major companies looking for expertise in user experience, eliminating the need for time-consuming outreach or bidding on projects.

5. **Becoming a Thought Leader**: By consistently sharing knowledge and participating in discussions, you can position yourself as a thought leader in your industry. Thought leadership can lead to speaking opportunities, media appearances, and invitations to contribute to high-profile projects or conferences. Becoming a thought leader adds credibility to your personal brand and makes you a go-to authority in your niche.

   o **Example**: A developer who frequently speaks at tech conferences and shares valuable insights on Twitter can become a recognized thought leader in the software development community, influencing industry trends and gaining career opportunities that align with their expertise.

Conclusion

In today's competitive tech industry, personal branding is not just a luxury—it's a necessity. By strategically building and promoting your personal brand, you can stand out in a crowded market, attract high-quality opportunities, and position yourself as an expert in your field. Whether you are just starting your career as a developer or looking to take your career to the next level, the power of personal branding will open doors that will shape your professional journey.

In the following chapters, we'll dive deeper into practical steps and real-world examples to help you craft and grow your personal brand as a developer. From building an online presence to engaging with communities and monetizing your expertise, this book will guide you every step of the way in standing out and advancing your career as a developer.

CHAPTER 2

UNDERSTANDING THE DEVELOPER LANDSCAPE

Overview of the Tech Industry and Its Growing Demand for Developers

The tech industry has experienced rapid growth over the last several decades, and this growth shows no signs of slowing down. Technology has become an integral part of nearly every aspect of modern life, from business operations to education, healthcare, entertainment, and communication. The demand for developers—individuals who can design, build, and maintain software solutions—has surged across every industry.

As technology continues to advance, the role of developers has become more critical than ever. Whether it's building websites, developing mobile apps, creating cloud-based solutions, or developing AI-driven systems, the need for developers is pervasive. According to multiple studies, the tech industry remains one of the fastest-growing sectors, with millions of new jobs being created each year for developers and other tech professionals. This growing demand means more opportunities for developers, but it also means increased competition.

For developers, this rapid demand offers significant career opportunities, but it also creates challenges. As more companies seek top talent, standing out and building a strong personal brand becomes essential for career growth. Personal branding allows developers to differentiate themselves in a crowded job market, showcasing not just their technical skills, but their unique value, approach, and expertise.

The global digital transformation across industries—from startups to large enterprises—has shifted many companies' focus to technology-driven solutions. As a result, developers are needed not just for traditional roles, but for positions involving emerging technologies such as blockchain, artificial intelligence, machine learning, Internet of Things (IoT), and more.

Real-world **Example**:
Companies like Google, Microsoft, and smaller startups have seen the demand for developers grow exponentially. For instance, the rapid development of cloud computing platforms, like AWS, Azure, and Google Cloud, has resulted

in a higher demand for developers with expertise in cloud technologies. This shift has created new opportunities for cloud developers to rise to the forefront of the tech industry.

Trends That Are Shaping the Future of Development and the Role of Personal Branding in These Shifts

As the tech industry evolves, several key trends are shaping the future of software development. Understanding these trends not only helps developers stay ahead of the curve but also provides opportunities to leverage personal branding to capitalize on new demands. Let's explore some of the most significant trends:

1. **The Rise of Artificial Intelligence and Machine Learning**:

   AI and machine learning are becoming more integrated into every industry, creating a growing need for developers who can work with these technologies. From natural language processing to self-driving cars, AI is expected to revolutionize multiple sectors, from healthcare to finance.

   How personal branding helps: As AI and machine learning continue to evolve, developers with expertise in these areas will be highly sought after. Building a personal brand around AI development or creating content that educates others on these topics can establish you as an expert in this rapidly expanding field.

2. **The Demand for Cybersecurity Experts**: With the rise of digital transformation, cyber threats are also growing, making cybersecurity one of the fastest-growing areas of development. Companies across all industries need skilled developers who can build secure systems and protect user data.

   How personal branding helps: Developers who specialize in cybersecurity and share their insights on social media or blogs will gain recognition in this critical field. By building a brand around security best practices and innovative security solutions, you can position yourself as a go-to expert for companies looking to safeguard their operations.

3. **The Expansion of Cloud Computing**: Cloud computing has rapidly become the backbone of many organizations' IT infrastructure, with platforms like Amazon Web Services (AWS),

Microsoft Azure, and Google Cloud leading the way. The migration to the cloud means more opportunities for developers who specialize in cloud platforms, DevOps, and serverless computing.

How personal branding helps: Developers with cloud computing skills are in high demand, and building a personal brand around cloud-based solutions can attract opportunities from global companies looking for cloud engineers and architects. By sharing cloud tutorials or offering advice on building cloud-native applications, you can establish your personal brand as one of expertise in this growing space.

4. **The Growth of Mobile and Web Applications**: The demand for mobile applications continues to rise as smartphones become an essential part of everyday life. Similarly, web applications remain critical for businesses to provide efficient services and reach customers. As the world continues to embrace mobile-first and web-first solutions, developers skilled in JavaScript, React Native, and progressive web apps are in demand.

How personal branding helps: Developers who focus on mobile and web technologies can build their brand by creating apps, sharing code snippets, and writing blog posts or tutorials that address common issues in mobile/web development. Demonstrating expertise through real-world projects and thought leadership in this area will set you apart from other developers.

5. **The Shift to Remote and Freelance Work**: Remote work has been a major trend for the past few years, and the COVID-19 pandemic accelerated this shift. Tech companies are increasingly offering remote positions, allowing developers to work with clients and teams from anywhere in the world. The rise of freelancing platforms like Upwork, Toptal, and Fiverr further demonstrates the flexibility in how developers can engage with clients.

How personal branding helps: Personal branding plays a significant role in freelancing and remote work, where competition is fierce. By cultivating a solid online presence—through platforms like LinkedIn, GitHub, and personal websites—you can attract clients from around the world. Showcasing

28

your work, testimonials, and contributions to open-source projects is an effective way to build credibility as a remote developer.

6. **Low-Code and No-Code Development**: Low-code and no-code platforms are transforming the way businesses develop applications. These platforms allow individuals with limited coding knowledge to create apps and websites, leading to greater demand for developers who can work alongside these tools, or enhance them with custom code.

How personal branding helps: As the use of no-code/low-code solutions grows, developers who understand how to integrate these tools with traditional development can create a niche for themselves. Sharing insights about how to extend these platforms or explaining how to integrate them with complex systems can attract clients looking for a hybrid approach.

Defining Your Unique Space as a Developer

As the demand for developers grows, the industry becomes more crowded, making it critical to define your unique space. Personal branding plays an essential role in carving out your niche and establishing yourself as an expert in your field. Here's how you can define and position yourself:

1. **Identify Your Passion and Expertise**: Consider what excites you most within development. Do you love building mobile apps, developing cloud solutions, working with data, or creating user interfaces? Finding your passion will allow you to focus your personal brand on a specific area, which is key to standing out in the industry.

   o **Real-life Example**: If you're passionate about AI development, your personal brand could center around building machine learning models, writing tutorials, and contributing to open-source AI projects. This helps you attract clients or employers who need AI expertise.

2. **Solve Specific Problems**: Developers who specialize in solving particular problems or addressing specific challenges can

30

distinguish themselves from generalist developers. For example, if you focus on creating fast, scalable APIs for startups, or specialize in creating secure cloud architectures for fintech companies, your personal brand can reflect that expertise.

- o **Real-life Example**: If your niche is database optimization for large-scale systems, you can create a blog and videos about optimizing SQL queries and building highly efficient databases. This will help potential clients or employers recognize you as the go-to person for that specific problem.

3. **Leverage Your Soft Skills**: In addition to technical expertise, soft skills like communication, leadership, and problem-solving can set you apart. By focusing on your unique combination of hard and soft skills, you can create a personal brand that is as much about your approach and work ethic as it is about your technical knowledge.

- o **Real-life Example**: A developer who is also an effective communicator might specialize in translating complex technical concepts into simple terms for non-technical clients.

This soft skill can make a developer indispensable, especially when working with non-tech teams or clients.

4. **Stay Current and Evolve**: Technology evolves rapidly, and so should your personal brand. Make it a point to stay updated with the latest technologies, trends, and industry shifts. Constantly evolving ensures that your brand remains relevant and continues to attract new opportunities.

   o **Real-life Example**: A developer focusing on mobile app development today might choose to pivot toward IoT (Internet of Things) development as the demand for connected devices grows. Updating your skill set and shifting your personal brand can position you as a leader in emerging tech.

Conclusion

The developer landscape is ever-changing, driven by technological advances and shifting market demands. By understanding the current trends and how personal branding can impact your career, you are in a stronger position to carve out your niche and stand out. Personal branding is a strategic tool for defining your unique space as a developer, attracting career opportunities, and positioning yourself as an expert. As the tech industry continues to grow, the developers who succeed will be those who invest in building and maintaining their personal brand, allowing them to grow alongside the industry and seize new opportunities as they arise.

In the next chapter, we will explore how to define your niche, develop your personal brand, and start positioning yourself as an expert in your specific area of development.

CHAPTER 3

DEFINING YOUR NICHE

How to Find and Specialize in a Niche Within the Developer Ecosystem

The tech industry is vast, with a wide range of technologies, tools, and services that developers can specialize in. From front-end development to machine learning, cloud computing, blockchain, and mobile development, the possibilities are endless. However, this broadness can be overwhelming, especially when you're just starting out. One of the most effective ways to stand out and build a successful personal brand is to find and specialize in a niche within the developer ecosystem.

Specializing in a niche allows you to differentiate yourself from other developers, making it easier to attract clients, employers, and collaborators who are looking for expertise in a specific area. Here's how you can find and specialize in a niche:

1. **Assess Your Interests and Passion**: Start by reflecting on the areas of development that

you enjoy the most. Are you more interested in building mobile apps, creating websites, or working with data? Understanding your passion is the first step in identifying a niche that will keep you motivated and excited about your work.

- o **Tip**: Think about the projects or technologies that have excited you the most in the past. For example, if you find yourself drawn to creating seamless user experiences, front-end development or UX/UI design might be a good niche for you.

2. **Analyze Your Strengths and Skills**: Evaluate your technical strengths and areas of expertise. Consider what skills you excel at and what technologies you are most proficient in. Whether it's a specific programming language, framework, or tool, these strengths can guide you toward a niche that suits your abilities.

- o **Tip**: If you're highly skilled in JavaScript, for example, you could specialize in frameworks like React or Node.js, which are highly in-demand in the industry.

3. **Research Market Demand**: While it's important to choose a niche that aligns

with your interests and skills, it's equally important to consider the market demand for that niche. Research what industries or sectors are actively looking for developers in specific areas. Are mobile app developers in high demand? Is there a growing need for blockchain developers? Identifying these trends can help you choose a niche that will offer long-term career opportunities.

   o **Tip**: Explore job boards, read industry reports, or check freelancing platforms like Upwork and Fiverr to see what types of developer skills are in demand.

4. **Look for Gaps in the Market**: As you research different niches, you may notice certain areas that are underrepresented or underserved. Identifying these gaps can give you a competitive advantage, as you can position yourself as one of the few experts in a growing area. For example, if there's a shortage of developers with expertise in augmented reality (AR) or machine learning for specific industries, this could be your chance to specialize in those fields.

   o **Tip**: Consider emerging technologies or industries that are not yet saturated, but are expected to grow in the coming years. This could be areas like AI for healthcare, or blockchain for supply chain management.

5. **Experiment and Learn**: Don't be afraid to experiment with different niches before settling on one. You can take on small projects or contribute to open-source projects in various areas to explore which one feels like the best fit. Over time, you'll naturally gravitate toward the niche that excites you and aligns with your skill set.

  o **Tip**: Create small side projects in different niches to test your interest and expertise. You could build a personal website, an app, or a game in a niche you're considering to see how much you enjoy working on it.

The Importance of Narrowing Down Your Focus for a Strong Personal Brand

One of the most common mistakes developers make is trying to be a "jack of all trades" and offering services in many different areas. While it may seem like a good idea to appeal to a broader audience, it can actually hinder your personal branding efforts. Here's why narrowing down your focus is crucial for building a strong personal brand:

1. **Clarity and Expertise**: Specializing in a niche allows you to clearly communicate your expertise to potential clients or employers. When you define your niche, people will instantly understand what you do and the value you offer. Being known for a specific skill or technology also helps you build authority in that area.

   o **Tip**: Instead of saying, "I'm a web developer," say, "I specialize in front-end development using React." This clarity makes it easier for others to understand what you do and how you can help them.

2. **Attracting the Right Clients**: By focusing on a niche, you attract clients or employers who specifically need your expertise. This makes it easier to find work that aligns with your interests and skill set, rather than taking on projects that are outside of your comfort zone or expertise.

   o **Tip**: A niche developer can charge higher rates because they provide specialized expertise. For example, a developer who specializes in building e-commerce websites on Shopify will be sought after by businesses that need that specific expertise.

3. **Building a Reputation**: The more focused your niche, the more opportunities you have to build a strong reputation. As you consistently produce high-quality work in your area of specialization, you'll develop a reputation as an expert in that field. This reputation will attract more clients, job offers, and opportunities.

   o **Tip**: Contribute to niche-related forums, write blog posts, and share your work on platforms like GitHub. These activities will help build your brand and reputation within your chosen niche.

4. **Differentiation in a Competitive Market**: With the growing number of developers in the industry, it's easy to get lost in the crowd. Specializing in a niche helps you stand out from the competition. Instead of competing with every other generalist developer, you're now positioning yourself as the go-to expert for a specific set of needs.

   o **Tip**: Identify your unique selling proposition (USP) within your niche. What makes you stand out compared to others in your field? Whether it's your approach, creativity, or technical skill, make sure your personal brand highlights this.

Real-World Examples of Successful Niche Developers

Here are some real-world examples of developers who have successfully defined their niche and built strong personal brands:

1. **Mobile** **Developers**: Mobile app development has become a popular niche, with iOS and Android developers in high demand. Developers who specialize in mobile development have the opportunity to work on a variety of exciting projects, from mobile games to enterprise apps.

   o **Example**: One developer may specialize in building iOS apps with Swift and have a strong personal brand around creating beautiful, user-friendly apps for startups. By focusing on this niche, they can attract clients in need of iOS expertise and build a strong reputation in the mobile app community.

2. **Cybersecurity** **Experts**: Cybersecurity is a rapidly growing field, with more

businesses seeking developers who can help protect their systems from data breaches, hacking, and other security threats. Developers who specialize in security can build their personal brand by offering consulting services, speaking at conferences, or writing about security best practices.

- o **Example**: A developer specializing in penetration testing or vulnerability assessments might build a reputation in the cybersecurity space by sharing vulnerability research, conducting workshops, and offering security audits to companies. This specialization can lead to consulting opportunities and higher-paying jobs.

3. **Blockchain Developers**: Blockchain technology has emerged as one of the most disruptive forces in tech. Developers who specialize in blockchain development, cryptocurrency systems, and smart contracts are in high demand. Blockchain developers can distinguish themselves by becoming experts in specific blockchain platforms, such as Ethereum, Solana, or Hyperledger.

41

- o **Example**: A developer who specializes in building decentralized applications (dApps) on Ethereum could build a personal brand by contributing to open-source blockchain projects, creating educational content, and speaking at blockchain-related events. This niche focus will make them stand out as a blockchain expert.

4. **Data Science and AI Developers**: As the demand for data-driven solutions grows, developers who specialize in data science, machine learning, and artificial intelligence are becoming highly sought after. These developers can use their expertise to solve complex problems and help businesses make data-driven decisions.

- o **Example**: A developer who specializes in machine learning algorithms for natural language processing (NLP) could create a strong personal brand by publishing research papers, teaching courses, and building NLP-related projects for businesses in fields like healthcare, finance, or e-commerce.

Conclusion

Defining your niche as a developer is one of the most important steps in building a successful personal brand. By focusing on a specific area of development, you can establish yourself as an expert, attract the right clients, and differentiate yourself from the competition. Whether you're passionate about mobile development, cybersecurity, blockchain, or any other niche, narrowing your focus allows you to stand out and build a brand that's recognized in your field.

In the next chapter, we'll explore how to effectively craft your personal brand and tell your unique story as a developer, setting you up for long-term success.

CHAPTER 4

SETTING CLEAR BRANDING GOALS

Why Goal Setting is Crucial for Developing Your Personal Brand

Setting clear branding goals is the foundation of building a successful personal brand. Without goals, your efforts can become scattered, and it becomes difficult to measure your progress or make informed decisions about your next steps. Personal branding, like any other professional development, requires focus, purpose, and direction. Goal setting gives you that clarity.

Here's why goal setting is essential for your personal brand development:

1. **Provides Direction and Focus**: Having clear goals helps you direct your energy and time toward actions that align with your brand vision. It ensures that you're not wasting effort on activities that don't support the overall mission of your personal brand.

     o **Example**: If your goal is to become a recognized expert in mobile app development, setting clear goals will help you prioritize actions like attending relevant conferences, writing blog posts, or contributing to open-source projects focused on mobile apps, rather than spreading yourself thin across unrelated tasks.

2. **Motivates and Drives Consistency**: Goals help keep you motivated, especially when working on long-term projects. They give you something tangible to strive for, which helps you push through challenges and maintain momentum over time. By having short-term milestones, you can celebrate progress and stay energized to work toward bigger, long-term achievements.

     o **Example**: A goal to publish one blog post per week on your developer blog creates a sense of accountability. Hitting this target every week builds consistency and keeps your brand visible.

3. **Helps You Stay Adaptable**: While goals provide focus, they also give you the flexibility to pivot or adjust when necessary. If

something isn't working or a new opportunity arises, well-defined goals allow you to make decisions based on what will best serve your brand in the long run.

- o **Example**: If you set a goal to increase your social media followers by 50% in six months but notice that creating video content on YouTube leads to higher engagement, you can adjust your approach to focus more on creating video content, while still aligning with your overarching goal of growing your online presence.

4. **Provides Measurable Results**: Personal branding goals give you a concrete way to measure your success. By defining specific, measurable outcomes, you can track your progress and adjust strategies to ensure continuous improvement. Success becomes less subjective and more data-driven.

- o **Example**: If your goal is to gain 1000 new followers on Twitter in three months, you can monitor your progress over time and make adjustments to your content strategy based on how close you are to achieving this goal.

Defining Short-Term and Long-Term Personal Branding Goals

Personal branding goals should be divided into short-term and long-term objectives. Short-term goals help you make immediate progress, while long-term goals provide a vision for where you want your personal brand to go in the future. Here's how to define each:

Short-Term Goals:

Short-term goals are typically achievable within a few weeks to months. They are the steps that lead to the larger picture and help you stay on track. Short-term goals are the building blocks of your personal brand and offer quick wins that boost your confidence and momentum.

1. **Examples of Short-Term Goals**:
   o Publish 2 blog posts about a niche topic (e.g., web development best practices) within the next month.
   o Increase your GitHub contributions by 30% in the next three months.

o Gain 500 new followers on LinkedIn or Twitter by engaging in daily discussions related to your niche.

o Attend one local developer meetup or webinar per month to build your network.

o Start creating video tutorials or coding livestreams every week for the next six weeks.

2. **How to Set Effective Short-Term Goals**:

o **Be Specific**: Instead of saying, "I want to grow my social media," set a goal like "I will grow my LinkedIn following by 10% in the next month by posting three times a week."

o **Be Achievable**: Make sure the goal is realistic given your current schedule and resources. A goal of attending a coding conference every week might not be feasible if you're just starting, but attending one every quarter might be more manageable.

o **Set Clear Deadlines**: Short-term goals should have specific timeframes that encourage urgency and focus. A deadline helps ensure you stay on track and avoid procrastination.

Long-Term Goals:

Long-term goals focus on where you want your personal brand to be in one to five years. These goals are broader and more strategic, such as becoming a thought leader in your field, landing a high-profile consulting gig, or publishing a book. Long-term goals provide a sense of direction, ensuring that your short-term efforts align with your larger vision.

1. **Examples of Long-Term Goals**:
    o Become a recognized speaker at three major tech conferences within the next two years.
    o Grow your personal brand to attract 10,000 followers on social media in the next year.
    o Launch your own online course on a specialized topic like machine learning in the next two years.
    o Secure a partnership with a top tech brand or startup as a consultant or advisor within five years.
    o Publish a technical book or eBook on a topic of expertise in the next three years.

2. **How to Set Effective Long-Term Goals**:
    o **Be Visionary**: Long-term goals are about the big picture. Think about where you want to

49

be in your career and what impact you want to have on the industry. The more visionary and inspiring your goal, the more it will drive you to take action.

- o **Make It Measurable**: Even though long-term goals are broader, they should still have measurable components. For example, you might want to become a thought leader in a certain programming language. Track your progress by the number of speaking opportunities, blog posts, or YouTube videos you publish over time.

- o **Break It Down**: While your long-term goal might seem distant, break it down into actionable short-term milestones. For example, if you want to become a keynote speaker at a major tech conference, you might break it down into smaller goals: attend local meetups, submit a talk proposal to a smaller conference, and build an online following.

Measuring Success and Tracking Progress

Measuring success and tracking progress are key components of goal setting. Without tracking, it's difficult to know if you're on track or if your efforts are yielding the desired results. Here's how to effectively track your personal branding goals:

1. **Use Analytics Tools**: Social media platforms like LinkedIn, Twitter, and GitHub provide built-in analytics that allow you to track your growth, engagement, and other key metrics. Use these tools to monitor your progress toward your social media growth goals.

   o **Tip**: Use tools like Google Analytics for your website or blog to track visitor traffic, page views, and how people are engaging with your content.

2. **Track Milestones**: Break down your short-term and long-term goals into smaller milestones and track your progress against them. For example, if your goal is to publish 10 blog posts in three months, track your progress every week to ensure you're staying on schedule.

   o **Tip**: Set monthly or quarterly check-ins to review your progress. Are you hitting your short-term goals? If not, identify what's holding you back and adjust your approach.

3. **Celebrate Achievements**: Every time you reach a milestone, celebrate your success. This boosts morale and keeps you motivated. Whether it's gaining 100 new followers or publishing your first blog post, small wins are important steps toward your larger vision.

   o **Tip**: Reward yourself when you meet a milestone. This doesn't have to be anything big—perhaps a short break, a celebratory lunch, or even sharing your success with your followers to reinforce the progress you've made.

4. **Adjust and Refine Goals**: Regularly assess your goals and progress. Sometimes, you may need to adjust your goals or methods if something isn't working. For instance, if your goal is to increase website traffic but the content isn't resonating with your audience, you might pivot your focus toward a different type of content or refine your messaging.

   o **Tip**: After every milestone, take time to reflect on what's working and what isn't. Don't be afraid to refine your goals and strategies as you learn more about what helps you build your personal brand.

Conclusion

Setting clear, actionable branding goals is essential to building and growing your personal brand as a developer. By defining both short-term and long-term goals, you provide yourself with direction, motivation, and measurable results. With the right goals in place, you'll not only track your progress but also make meaningful strides toward becoming a recognized expert in your niche.

In the next chapter, we'll discuss how to craft and tell your developer story, a crucial element in differentiating yourself and making your personal brand more relatable and authentic to your audience.

CHAPTER 5

CRAFTING YOUR DEVELOPER STORY

The Power of Storytelling in Personal Branding

Storytelling is one of the most powerful tools in building a personal brand. As a developer, your technical skills are important, but your story is what makes you memorable. It's how you connect with your audience on a deeper, more personal level. Stories are how we make sense of the world and how we relate to others. When it comes to personal branding, your story can set you apart, making you stand out among countless other developers in a competitive field.

Storytelling allows you to:

- **Humanize your brand**: Behind every developer is a person with unique experiences, challenges, and successes. Sharing your personal story allows others to relate to you as a person, not just as a skillset.
- **Create emotional connections**: A well-crafted story can create an emotional connection with your audience. People remember stories more than facts

54

or skills, and they are more likely to follow or hire someone they feel personally connected to.

- **Showcase your journey**: Personal branding is about showcasing how you got to where you are now. Storytelling lets you highlight the obstacles you've overcome, the lessons you've learned, and how you've grown as a developer, which adds authenticity to your brand.

A great developer story makes you more than just a name and a list of technologies—it turns you into a memorable individual that people want to work with, collaborate with, or follow.

How to Craft a Compelling Personal Story That Resonates with Your Audience

Crafting a compelling personal story is about authenticity, relatability, and consistency. Your story should reflect who you are as a person and as a developer, while also addressing your audience's needs or interests. Here's how to create a personal story that resonates with your audience:

1. **Define Your 'Why'**: Every good story has a core purpose or mission—

your "why." Ask yourself: Why did you become a developer? What motivates you to build software, write code, or contribute to the tech community? This central theme will guide your story and make it relatable to others in similar situations.

- o **Example**: Maybe you started coding as a way to solve a problem you were facing personally, like building an app to track your fitness goals. Your story could center around how your passion for solving real-world problems led you into development.

2. **Highlight Key Moments and Challenges**: Every good story has a beginning, middle, and end. To make your story compelling, focus on key moments in your career or personal life that led you to where you are today. These might include challenges you faced (and overcame), pivotal decisions you made, or experiences that shaped your development journey. Highlighting these moments makes your story more relatable and memorable.

- o **Example**: You might share how you initially struggled with learning a programming language, but through persistence and finding the right community resources, you became proficient in it. This struggle, followed by your growth, creates a narrative of perseverance.

3. **Show Your Growth and Learning**: One of the most important aspects of your developer story is showcasing how you've grown. Personal growth resonates with audiences because it's a shared experience. Whether it's learning new skills, taking on challenging projects, or evolving your understanding of software development, showing how you've grown will help others connect with your journey.

   o **Example**: Perhaps you started as a self-taught developer learning through online tutorials, then transitioned to building your own projects or contributing to open-source. Highlighting this journey of self-improvement gives your audience a clear sense of progression and shows your commitment to development.

4. **Incorporate the Human Element**: Personal stories are more than just about professional achievements; they also include the human element—your emotions, motivations, and values.

Make your story relatable by sharing the challenges you faced (e.g., balancing a day job with learning to code, overcoming imposter syndrome, or the excitement of landing your first freelance gig). Authenticity is key to making your story resonate.

- o **Example**: If you've ever faced imposter syndrome or dealt with setbacks, sharing that vulnerability in your story can humanize you. It makes you more approachable and shows that, like others, you've faced difficulties but overcame them.

5. **Align Your Story with Your Brand Goals**: Your personal story should align with your brand's vision and mission. If your goal is to position yourself as an expert in mobile development, your story should highlight how you became passionate about mobile apps, the projects you've worked on, and how you've continuously refined your skills in that area. Make sure that your story supports your brand's messaging and strengthens your overall narrative.

- o **Example**: If you aim to be known for your expertise in backend development, your story should emphasize your work with databases,

APIs, and server-side programming. You can showcase specific projects where you solved complex backend challenges, and explain how this experience contributes to your unique value as a developer.

6. **Keep It Concise and Engaging**: While storytelling is powerful, it's important to keep your personal brand story concise and engaging. Avoid overwhelming your audience with excessive details. Focus on the most impactful parts of your journey that relate to your brand message. Your story should capture attention quickly and keep your audience interested throughout.

   o **Example**: A short story about how you went from building small web projects for friends to working with clients on complex systems is both engaging and clear. Avoid unnecessary tangents or long-winded explanations that might distract from the core message.

Real-World Examples of Developers Who Have Successfully
Told Their Stories

Here are some real-world examples of developers who have effectively told their stories and used those stories to build strong personal brands:

1. **John Sonmez (Simple Programmer)**: John Sonmez, a well-known developer and author of the "Soft Skills" book series, used storytelling to build a personal brand around helping developers improve not only their coding skills but their careers as a whole. His story about overcoming challenges and transitioning from being a frustrated developer to a successful entrepreneur resonated with his audience. By sharing his personal journey of success and failure, he was able to position himself as a mentor and leader in the developer community.

   o **Key Takeaway**: John effectively used his story to build trust and connect with developers on a deeper level, making his brand about personal growth and career success, not just coding skills.

2. **Sarah Drasner (SVG Animation Expert)**: Sarah Drasner is an expert in SVG animation and a

prominent figure in the front-end development community. She has shared her personal story of being a self-taught developer, navigating the challenges of learning new skills, and ultimately becoming a recognized leader in the field of animations. Her story of persistence and growth has resonated with many developers, especially those starting their journeys or struggling to overcome obstacles.

- o **Key Takeaway**: Sarah's story emphasizes the importance of self-learning, perseverance, and finding a niche. She has effectively used her story to brand herself as an expert in SVG animations, making her more relatable to aspiring developers in the front-end space.

3. **Chris Coyier (CSS-Tricks)**: Chris Coyier is the founder of CSS-Tricks and co-founder of CodePen. His personal brand story revolves around his passion for front-end web development, and how he transformed his knowledge into a widely respected resource for other developers. His story includes his journey from a freelance web designer to a content creator and

61

entrepreneur, highlighting the lessons he learned along the way.

- o **Key Takeaway**: Chris uses storytelling to show how his work on CSS-Tricks and CodePen was driven by his desire to help others learn and improve their front-end skills. His story is a testament to the power of giving back to the community and establishing authority through consistent content creation.

4. **Mosh Hamedani (Code with Mosh)**: Mosh Hamedani is a software engineer and online instructor who has built a personal brand around teaching coding and software development. His story is about transitioning from working in corporate software development to becoming an online educator. He shares his experiences of what it was like to start teaching others and the challenges he faced in creating his platform.

- o **Key Takeaway**: Mosh's story about moving from being an employee to an educator highlights the importance of persistence and adaptability. He also exemplifies the power of finding your niche (software development education) and leveraging your expertise to help others.

Conclusion

Crafting your developer story is a crucial part of building your personal brand. It allows you to share your journey, experiences, and unique perspective, helping you connect with your audience on a personal level. A compelling story humanizes your brand, makes you memorable, and sets you apart in a competitive industry. By reflecting on your "why," highlighting your challenges and growth, and aligning your story with your brand goals, you can create a narrative that resonates with others and supports your career advancement.

In the next chapter, we will explore how to develop your online presence and optimize your profiles on platforms like LinkedIn, GitHub, and personal websites to support and amplify your personal brand story.

CHAPTER 6

DEVELOPING YOUR ONLINE PRESENCE

Why a Strong Online Presence is Essential for Personal Branding

In today's digital age, your online presence is your virtual first impression. Whether you're looking to connect with potential clients, network with fellow developers, or seek job opportunities, your online presence is often the first thing people will look at. A well-crafted and consistent online presence is a key factor in building a strong personal brand. Here's why having a solid online presence is essential for developers:

1. **Visibility and Accessibility**: A strong online presence ensures that you're easily found by potential employers, clients, and collaborators. When you're active online, whether it's through social media, your blog, or coding platforms, people are more likely to come across your work and expertise. Without an online presence,

you may be missing out on opportunities simply because people don't know you exist.

- o **Example**: A developer who regularly shares tutorials, blog posts, or projects on GitHub and LinkedIn increases their chances of being discovered by companies looking for talent in that particular technology stack.

2. **Showcase of Expertise**: Online platforms, especially GitHub and personal blogs, are a place where you can showcase your technical skills, projects, and contributions. This not only highlights your abilities but also builds credibility and authority in your field. Clients, employers, or even collaborators can assess your expertise by viewing your public work.

- o **Example**: A developer who contributes to open-source projects on GitHub or shares their coding journey on a blog shows their dedication to continuous learning and contributes to the development community, enhancing their professional reputation.

3. **Networking Opportunities**: Building an online presence creates opportunities for networking with fellow developers, mentors, clients,

or thought leaders. Participating in forums, discussions, and collaborative projects online can open doors to new career opportunities, collaborations, and partnerships.

- o **Example**: Engaging in technical communities on platforms like Stack Overflow or Twitter allows you to build relationships with like-minded professionals and establish your name in the industry. Networking can often lead to job offers, freelance opportunities, or valuable collaborations.

4. **Trust and Authenticity**: A consistent online presence also helps build trust with your audience. By regularly contributing valuable content, engaging with others in your community, and demonstrating your knowledge, you showcase not only your skills but also your reliability and commitment to your field.

- o **Example**: A developer who actively participates in coding challenges or shares useful resources online will be seen as someone who's genuinely interested in advancing both their own skills and helping others.

How to Optimize Your LinkedIn Profile, GitHub, and Other Platforms

To maximize your online presence, it's crucial to optimize your profiles across platforms like LinkedIn, GitHub, personal websites, and social media. Here's how you can make the most out of these platforms:

LinkedIn Profile Optimization

LinkedIn is one of the most important platforms for professional networking, so it's essential to ensure your profile is polished and professional.

1. **Professional Profile Picture**: Your LinkedIn profile picture is the first thing people see. Choose a clear, professional photo that represents you well in a work context. Avoid casual photos, and make sure you're dressed appropriately for your industry.
   - **Tip**: A well-lit photo with a simple background, where you're smiling or looking approachable, is ideal.

2. **Compelling   Headline**: Your headline should go beyond just your job title. It should reflect what you do and what makes you unique. Include keywords that will make it easy for others to find you. For example, "Full-Stack Developer | JavaScript & React Expert | Passionate About Building Scalable Web Apps" clearly defines who you are and what you specialize in.

   o **Tip**: Use keywords relevant to your skills and niche to ensure your profile appears in searches for those looking for your expertise.

3. **Detailed   Experience   and   Skills**: List your relevant work experience, but go further than just listing job responsibilities. Describe your accomplishments, the projects you worked on, and the technologies you used. Tailor your descriptions to reflect how you've added value at each job or project.

   o **Tip**: Use bullet points for clarity and include quantifiable results if possible (e.g., "Reduced page load time by 30% through optimized JavaScript code").

4. **Showcase   Your   Work**: Add links to your GitHub repositories, personal

projects, or any publications you've worked on. This gives recruiters and potential clients an opportunity to see examples of your work.

- o **Tip**: Link to code samples, live apps, or even blog posts that demonstrate your skills and experience.

5. **Engage and Network**: LinkedIn is a social platform, so it's important to engage with others. Share relevant content, comment on posts, and connect with others in your field. This helps increase your visibility and expands your network.

- o **Tip**: Follow industry leaders, join relevant groups, and contribute to discussions to stay engaged and visible within your community.

GitHub Optimization

GitHub is one of the most important platforms for developers. It's where you showcase your coding work, contributions, and projects. Here's how to make your GitHub profile stand out:

1. **Organize Your Repositories**: Make sure your repositories are well-organized,

clearly named, and contain appropriate descriptions. Showcase your best work by pinning your most impressive projects at the top of your profile.

- o **Tip**: Add clear, concise READMEs to your projects to explain what they do and how others can use or contribute to them.

2. **Contribute to Open-Source Projects**: Contributing to open-source projects is a great way to showcase your skills, build your reputation, and give back to the developer community. It demonstrates your willingness to collaborate and improve the software ecosystem.

- o **Tip**: Look for open-source projects that align with your skills or interests and start by tackling open issues or bugs.

3. **Showcase Completed Projects**: For personal projects, make sure your code is well-documented, clean, and fully functional. Provide context around the project—why you built it, what technologies were used, and any challenges you overcame.

- o **Tip**: Use GitHub Pages to host a live demo of your projects if applicable, or link to a hosted version of the app so visitors can easily try it out.

4. **Engage with the Community**: Engage with other developers by starring projects, following others, and commenting on repositories. This can help you gain visibility and connect with others in the developer community.

   o **Tip**: Participate in GitHub discussions and issues, share feedback on projects, and contribute to collaborations to boost your presence.

Other Platforms: Personal Website, Twitter, Medium, and Stack Overflow

1. **Personal Website**: Your personal website is your digital business card. It's the best place to showcase your portfolio, blog posts, achievements, and a brief introduction to who you are and what you do. It's also the perfect place to share your resume and contact information.

   o **Tip**: Keep your website simple and professional. Include your best work and make sure it's easy to navigate.

2. **Twitter**:

Twitter is a great platform for developers to stay connected with the latest industry trends, share insights, and network with other developers. Your Twitter profile can be a great extension of your personal brand, showcasing your thoughts on technology, development, and the industry.

- o **Tip**: Engage in conversations, share useful content, and participate in relevant hashtags like #100DaysOfCode to build a following and engage with others in the community.

3. **Medium**:

Writing blog posts on Medium or a personal blog is a fantastic way to share your knowledge and demonstrate your expertise. Writing technical articles about tools, frameworks, or coding challenges you've overcome can establish your authority and help others in the community.

- o **Tip**: Write practical, beginner-friendly articles that solve common problems or provide value to other developers. Consistently publishing content will build your personal brand as an expert.

4. **Stack** **Overflow**:
Stack Overflow is a go-to platform for developers looking to ask or answer technical questions. By contributing regularly, you not only help others but also showcase your knowledge and skills, which can attract opportunities.

   o **Tip**: Focus on answering questions in your niche to build a reputation as an expert in that area. Make sure your answers are clear, thorough, and helpful.

The Do's and Don'ts of Social Media Profiles for Developers

To maintain a professional image while leveraging social media to build your brand, here are some key do's and don'ts:

Do's:

- **Do Maintain Professionalism**: Keep your profiles professional while still reflecting your personality. Your social media presence should be an extension of your personal brand, demonstrating your expertise while engaging with your audience.

- **Do Share Value**: Share useful content, tips, tutorials, and resources that will benefit others in your community. This positions you as a helpful and knowledgeable developer.

- **Do Be Consistent**: Make sure your message and tone are consistent across all platforms. Use the same professional photo, similar bio descriptions, and consistently share content that supports your personal brand.

Don'ts:

- **Don't Over-Post Personal Content**: While it's okay to show some personality, social media profiles should focus on professional content. Avoid posting overly personal details or controversial opinions that might harm your reputation.

- **Don't Neglect Your Profile**: An outdated or incomplete profile can give a negative impression. Regularly update your LinkedIn, GitHub, and other profiles to reflect your latest work, skills, and accomplishments.

- **Don't Be Negative**: Negative comments, complaints, or toxic behavior on social media can damage your personal brand. Stay positive, professional, and constructive when engaging with others online.

Conclusion

Developing a strong online presence is key to building and growing your personal brand as a developer. By optimizing your LinkedIn profile, GitHub repositories, personal website, and other platforms, you can effectively showcase your skills, attract opportunities, and network with others in the tech community. Consistency, professionalism, and value sharing are essential to growing your brand and establishing yourself as an authority in your niche.

In the next chapter, we will dive into the importance of content creation and how producing valuable resources—like blogs, videos, and tutorials—can help expand your personal brand and reach a wider audience.

CHAPTER 7

BUILDING A PERSONAL WEBSITE OR PORTFOLIO

Why Having a Personal Website is a Must for Developers

In today's digital world, a personal website is more than just an online resume—it's your digital identity. As a developer, your website serves as the central hub for your personal brand, showcasing your skills, projects, and expertise in a professional and easily accessible format. Here's why having a personal website is essential for developers:

1. **Centralized Location for Your Work**: A personal website is a one-stop destination where potential clients, employers, and collaborators can learn about you and view your work. Whether you're a freelancer, a job seeker, or an entrepreneur, your website serves as your digital portfolio, offering a place to host everything from code samples and project demos to blog posts and tutorials.

    o **Example**: Instead of directing potential clients to various social media platforms or GitHub repositories, your website provides a clean and organized space for them to easily access your contact information, projects, and achievements.

2. **Professionalism and Credibility**: A well-designed website adds a layer of professionalism to your personal brand. It shows that you're serious about your career and committed to presenting yourself as a polished professional. It builds trust and credibility in a way that LinkedIn or GitHub profiles alone cannot.

   o **Example**: Having a custom domain (e.g., www.johndoe.dev) makes you look more professional than using a generic service like a GitHub page URL (e.g., github.io/username).

3. **SEO and Discoverability**: Your personal website can be optimized for search engines, making it easier for people to find you online. With the right keywords, a well-structured site, and regular content updates, you can increase your chances of ranking on search engines like Google, which boosts your online visibility.

   o **Example**: If you specialize in web development, you can optimize your site to rank for keywords like "React.js developer" or "full-stack web development," helping potential employers or clients find you through organic search.

4. **Control Over Your Brand and Content**: Unlike social media profiles or platforms like LinkedIn, a personal website allows you full control over how you present your brand. You can customize your design, content, and messaging to reflect your personality, work style, and niche in the tech industry.

   o **Example**: You can decide to have a minimalist design or a dynamic, interactive portfolio that shows off your front-end development skills. You also have the freedom to share specific projects and content that align with your brand vision.

What to Include in Your Portfolio to Attract the Right Attention

A developer portfolio should do more than just list your skills; it should demonstrate your abilities, highlight your achievements, and showcase the value you can bring to clients or employers. Here's what to include in your portfolio to make a strong impact:

1. **A Clear, Professional Introduction**: Your portfolio should start with a brief, engaging introduction that explains who you are, what you do, and what makes you unique as a developer. This is your chance to provide a snapshot of your skills, your values, and your passion for tech.

   o **Tip**: Include a clear headline like "Full-Stack Developer | Specializing in React and Node.js" followed by a short paragraph that provides more detail about your background and what drives you.

2. **Showcase Your Best Work**: The core of your portfolio should be the projects you've worked on. Focus on quality, not quantity—choose a few standout projects that best demonstrate your skills and problem-solving abilities. Include detailed descriptions of each project, along with the technologies you used and any challenges you faced.

   o **Tip**: For each project, include a link to the live version (if applicable) and the source code on GitHub. A well-documented case study with a description of your approach will provide valuable insight into your process.

3. **Skills and Technologies**: Clearly list the technologies and tools you are proficient in. This section helps recruiters, clients, and collaborators quickly see if your skillset matches their needs. Be honest about your level of expertise (e.g., "Intermediate in JavaScript" vs. "Expert in React").

   o **Tip**: Consider using icons or a visual representation to make this section easy to read and scan. You can include programming languages, frameworks, tools, and platforms you work with, such as "React.js," "Node.js," "AWS," etc.

4. **Client Testimonials or References**: Including testimonials from previous clients or colleagues adds credibility and social proof to your portfolio. Positive feedback can reassure potential clients or employers that you're a reliable and skilled developer. If you're just starting out, consider including endorsements from classmates, mentors, or collaborators.

o **Tip**: Even if you're just starting out, consider asking for feedback from clients you've worked with on small projects, or from any contributors you've worked with on open-source initiatives.

5. **Blog or Educational Content**: Having a blog or contributing to technical writing can showcase your thought leadership and demonstrate your expertise. Sharing tutorials, problem-solving tips, or insights about development challenges shows you're engaged with the community and can communicate complex topics clearly.

o **Tip**: Regularly update your blog with content relevant to your niche or areas of expertise. If you're a front-end developer, for example, write about JavaScript frameworks, UI/UX design principles, or performance optimization.

6. **A Contact Page**: Make it easy for potential clients, employers, or collaborators to contact you. Include a clear call to action (CTA) with your email address, a contact

81

form, or links to your professional social media profiles like LinkedIn or Twitter.

- o **Tip**: Keep your contact information easy to find on every page (typically in the header or footer) to make it as accessible as possible.

7. **Resume or CV**: Many visitors to your portfolio will want to see your formal resume or CV. Include an up-to-date version on your site, or at least offer a downloadable PDF version. Keep it concise, focusing on your relevant experience and skills.

- o **Tip**: Make sure your resume is tailored to your career goals and highlights your most relevant accomplishments, projects, and experiences.

8. **Interactive Elements or Demos**: As a developer, you have the opportunity to showcase your work in interactive ways. If possible, add live demos, code samples, or interactive elements to your portfolio to demonstrate your skills directly.

- o **Tip**: Include a section where users can interact with small projects (e.g., an interactive web app or a code snippet) to better showcase your abilities.

Examples of Standout Developer Portfolios and Websites

Here are some examples of developer portfolios that stand out due to their design, functionality, and content:

1. **Timothy Jordan** (timothyjordan.com): Timothy's website is a great example of a developer's personal brand in action. He uses his site to showcase his portfolio, skills, and projects, with an interactive design that highlights his expertise in web development and his work in the tech community. His clean, easy-to-navigate design and well-written content make it easy to understand his value proposition.

2. **Brittany Chiang** (brittanychiang.com): Brittany's portfolio website is an excellent example of an interactive, visually appealing design. She showcases a series of personal projects and open-source contributions, with detailed case studies and links to the live projects and source code. The design is minimalistic and professional, and it clearly

demonstrates her expertise in front-end development, with a focus on React.

3. **Adham Dannaway** (adhamdannaway.com): Adham's personal website features a unique, creative design that stands out from the crowd. He includes several interactive elements and showcases a variety of projects in different domains, from UX design to web development. His site serves as both a portfolio and a demonstration of his skills in building visually stunning websites.

4. **Devon Morrison** (devonmorrison.dev): Devon's portfolio website is simple but effective. It uses bold typography and a clear layout to communicate who he is, his skills, and the projects he's worked on. The website also includes a clean, easy-to-read resume section, making it easy for potential employers to learn about his professional experience.

5. **João Ribeiro** (joaoribeiro.dev): João's site is an excellent example of a developer who has effectively used his website to showcase his work and expertise. The site features a minimalist design with strong visuals, and his case studies are well-organized and easy to navigate. He also

includes a blog section where he shares valuable technical insights and tutorials.

Conclusion

A personal website and portfolio are essential for building your personal brand as a developer. Your website not only serves as a hub for showcasing your skills, but it also provides an opportunity to demonstrate your professionalism, creativity, and dedication to your craft. By including relevant projects, a clear introduction, client testimonials, and educational content, you can create a portfolio that effectively communicates your value to potential clients, employers, and collaborators.

In the next chapter, we will explore the importance of creating content—such as blogs, tutorials, and videos—to further enhance your personal brand and share your knowledge with the developer community.

CHAPTER 8

WRITING TECHNICAL BLOG POSTS

How Writing Blog Posts Can Elevate Your Personal Brand

Blogging is an excellent way for developers to showcase their expertise, share knowledge, and connect with a wider audience. Writing technical blog posts helps establish you as a thought leader in your field, boosts your visibility, and provides value to your audience. Here's how writing blog posts can elevate your personal brand:

1. **Demonstrating Expertise**: By writing about the technologies you use and the challenges you've overcome, you demonstrate your knowledge and problem-solving skills. When you publish high-quality content on a consistent basis, your audience comes to recognize you as an expert in your area of specialization.

   o **Example**: If you specialize in web development, writing about advanced topics such as React, Node.js, or front-end architecture will showcase your technical skills and draw attention from potential employers or clients.

2. **Building   Credibility**: Regularly publishing blog posts helps you build credibility in the tech community. As you share your experiences, insights, and solutions to common problems, readers will begin to trust you as a reliable resource for valuable information.

   o **Example**: A blog post on how you solved a complex bug in your code or improved performance in a web app can provide real-world value to other developers, establishing you as someone who provides actionable insights.

3. **Attracting   New   Opportunities**: Writing blog posts can open doors to new opportunities, such as job offers, speaking engagements, and freelance gigs. When people read your posts, they may reach out to you for collaboration, consulting, or to hire you for a project. A well-maintained blog also serves as a portfolio of your work that potential employers or clients can reference.

- o **Example**: If you write a compelling blog post on building scalable cloud applications, companies in need of cloud developers might contact you to offer freelance work or a full-time position.

4. **Improving Your Communication Skills**: Writing blog posts forces you to articulate complex concepts in a clear and understandable way. This improves your communication skills, which are essential for both collaboration and client-facing roles. Writing is a great way to practice explaining technical topics to non-technical audiences, making you more versatile as a developer.

   - o **Example**: Writing about complex topics such as APIs, data structures, or machine learning helps you refine your ability to explain technical information in simple, digestible terms, which is valuable when communicating with teams or clients.

5. **Increasing Visibility and Online Presence**: A blog is a fantastic way to increase your online visibility. By writing content relevant to your niche, you can rank for keywords on search engines, making it easier for people to find you. It's a great

way to enhance your SEO, which helps attract more traffic to your website or portfolio.

- o **Example**: If you write about Python or web development best practices, and optimize your blog posts for search engines, people searching for solutions to common programming problems are more likely to find your content.

Topics to Write About and How to Make Your Posts Engaging

Writing blog posts that resonate with your audience is key to building an engaged readership. Here are some ideas for blog topics and tips on making your posts both informative and engaging:

Popular Topics for Developer Blogs

1. **Tutorials and How-Tos**: Tutorials are one of the most popular types of blog posts among developers. People are always looking for solutions to specific problems or learning resources. Writing step-by-step guides on how to build apps, integrate APIs, or use certain frameworks

will attract readers who are looking for practical help.

  o **Example**: "How to Build a Real-Time Chat App with React and Firebase" or "Step-by-Step Guide to Deploying a Node.js App on Heroku."

2. **Case   Studies**:

Case studies are a great way to showcase real-world applications of your skills. Write about projects you've worked on, the challenges you faced, the solutions you implemented, and the results. Case studies demonstrate your problem-solving abilities and give readers a behind-the-scenes look at how you approach development.

  o **Example**: "How I Optimized the Performance of a React App by 40%" or "Building a Scalable Backend for a Growing E-Commerce Store."

3. **Technical   Deep   Dives**:

If you have expertise in a specific technology or framework, write in-depth articles about how it works and the best practices for using it. These posts help you demonstrate deep knowledge and give value to developers who are looking to learn more about the technology.

- o **Example**: "Understanding How React's Virtual DOM Works" or "A Deep Dive into Kubernetes for DevOps Engineers."

4. **Industry Insights and Trends**: Share your thoughts on industry trends, new technologies, or emerging tools. This can position you as a thought leader who is ahead of the curve. Writing about what's happening in the tech world shows that you are engaged with the industry and keeps your audience informed.

- o **Example**: "The Future of AI in Web Development" or "Why Serverless Architecture is Changing How We Build Apps."

5. **Opinion Pieces or Experiences**: Opinion pieces give you the chance to share your personal experiences, challenges, and lessons learned. Writing about your journey as a developer, the challenges you've overcome, or your views on best practices can help humanize your brand and build a connection with your readers.

○ **Example**: "Why I Switched from Freelancing to a Full-Time Developer Role" or "The Biggest Mistakes I've Made as a Self-Taught Developer."

How to Make Your Blog Posts Engaging

1. **Keep It Simple and Readable**: Break up your content into short paragraphs and use headers, bullet points, and code snippets to make it easier to read. Developers are often pressed for time, so readability is key. Use clear and concise language to ensure that your posts are easily digestible.

   ○ **Tip**: Use visual aids like screenshots or diagrams to explain complex concepts. This can help readers understand your ideas better and break up long text.

2. **Use Examples and Code Snippets**: Including real-world examples or code snippets in your blog posts can make the content more practical and actionable. Developers love to see how things work in practice, and code snippets provide concrete examples that readers can use directly in their own work.

    o **Tip**: Make sure your code is properly formatted and easy to understand. Use tools like GitHub Gists or embed code directly into your blog to make it easy for readers to copy and test.

3. **Engage with Your Audience**: Encourage comments and feedback from your readers by asking questions at the end of your blog posts or inviting them to share their experiences. Respond to comments and engage with your readers to build a community around your blog.

    o **Tip**: At the end of your posts, ask readers to share their thoughts or tell you about their experiences with the topic. For example, "What challenges have you faced while working with React?" or "Do you agree with my thoughts on the future of AI in development?"

4. **Be Authentic and Personal**: Don't be afraid to share your personal experiences, opinions, and insights. Authenticity is what makes your content unique and relatable. Let your personality shine through your writing to create a

more engaging and memorable experience for your readers.

- o **Tip**: Share personal anecdotes, such as "The first time I built a production-level app, I faced a huge issue with X, but I learned a valuable lesson from it."

Real-World Examples of Developers Who Gained Recognition Through Blogging

Here are some real-world examples of developers who have successfully used blogging to build their personal brand and gain recognition:

1. **Kent   C.   Dodds**
   Kent C. Dodds is a well-known React and JavaScript developer, educator, and author. He gained recognition through his blog and open-source contributions, particularly his blog posts about testing, React development, and JavaScript best practices. His content has helped countless developers learn and improve their skills, and he has built a strong personal brand around teaching and mentoring.

94

- o **Key Takeaway**: Kent's blog content is educational, focused on helping developers solve real problems, which has led to his recognition in the React community.

2. **Dan   Abramov**

Dan Abramov, co-author of Redux and a key figure in the React ecosystem, has built a strong brand through his blog and writing. His blog posts on React and JavaScript best practices have been highly influential in the developer community. His ability to break down complex concepts into digestible pieces has made his work widely respected.

- o **Key Takeaway**: Dan's blog posts and writing on topics that interest him have solidified his position as a thought leader in the React and JavaScript community.

3. **Mosh   Hamedani**

Mosh Hamedani, a software engineer and online instructor, has used blogging and content creation to build a personal brand and launch his own online courses. His tutorials and blog posts on topics like C#, React, and Node.js are widely followed by developers looking to improve their skills.

- o **Key Takeaway**: Mosh's blog serves as both a portfolio and a platform for sharing educational content. His focus on creating content that adds value to his audience has helped him build a large following.

4. **Sarah**   **Drasner**

Sarah Drasner, a front-end engineer and educator, has used blogging and writing to build her brand as an expert in web animation and SVG graphics. Her blog posts are educational, often explaining complex animations in a simple and approachable way.

- o **Key Takeaway**: Sarah's ability to simplify complicated topics and her focus on providing actionable content have earned her recognition in the front-end development community.

Conclusion

Writing technical blog posts is one of the most effective ways to elevate your personal brand as a developer. By sharing your knowledge, experiences, and insights, you can establish yourself as a thought leader, build credibility, and attract new career opportunities. Whether you're writing tutorials, sharing case studies, or offering opinions on industry trends, blogging helps you showcase your expertise and connect with a wider audience.

In the next chapter, we will explore how to optimize your social media presence and effectively network within the tech community to amplify your personal brand.

CHAPTER 9

CREATING AND SHARING OPEN-SOURCE PROJECTS

The Role of Open-Source Contributions in Building Your Personal Brand

Open-source contributions are one of the most powerful ways to build your personal brand as a developer. Contributing to open-source projects not only allows you to give back to the community, but it also serves as a highly visible way to showcase your skills, problem-solving abilities, and commitment to continuous learning. Here's how open-source contributions play a key role in developing your personal brand:

1. **Showcase Your Expertise**: When you contribute to open-source projects, you're essentially showcasing your knowledge and expertise for the world to see. You have the opportunity to solve real-world problems, write clean code, and collaborate with developers from around the globe. These contributions demonstrate your

technical abilities, making you more attractive to potential employers or clients.

- o **Example**: By contributing a feature or fixing bugs in a popular open-source project like React or Vue.js, you gain recognition from developers and organizations that rely on these frameworks.

2. **Increase Your Visibility**: Open-source projects are widely visible and have broad community support. Your contributions are often reviewed, discussed, and even promoted by others in the community. This not only boosts your reputation but also makes you a part of a global network of developers who respect your work.

- o **Example**: A pull request that gets merged into a popular repository might get attention from developers worldwide, increasing your visibility and positioning you as an authority in that particular technology or framework.

3. **Create a Portfolio of Work**: Your open-source contributions act as a portfolio of your coding skills. By participating in open-source projects, you create a public record of your work that others can see, evaluate, and reference. This portfolio

becomes an integral part of your personal brand, showcasing not just your technical abilities but your passion for software development.

- o **Example**: A GitHub profile with several well-documented contributions to projects, along with your own repositories, can serve as a comprehensive showcase of your coding style and expertise.

4. **Establish Thought Leadership**: Contributing to open-source projects and writing about them (e.g., blog posts, tutorials, or case studies) can help position you as a thought leader. Open-source contributions allow you to demonstrate not just your technical skills but also your ability to communicate effectively with others. Thought leadership can increase your influence in the tech community and create more opportunities for you.

- o **Example**: If you write a blog post explaining how you solved a difficult bug in an open-source project, others in the community will learn from your experience, and your name will become associated with that solution.

How to Start Contributing to Open-Source and Why It's Beneficial for Career Growth

Getting started with open-source contributions can be a bit intimidating, but once you understand how it works and the many benefits it offers, you'll see how valuable it is for your personal and professional growth. Here's how you can start contributing to open-source and why it's crucial for your career development:

Steps to Start Contributing

1. **Find Projects That Align with Your Interests**: Start by identifying open-source projects that align with your interests, expertise, or the technologies you want to learn. GitHub is an excellent place to explore a wide range of open-source repositories, from beginner-friendly projects to more advanced contributions. You can search for projects using tags or explore repositories related to specific programming languages or frameworks.

   o **Tip**: Look for projects that have a "good first issue" label. These are usually beginner-friendly issues that are easy to start with and are designed to help new contributors get involved.

2. **Start** **Small**: As a beginner, it's best to start with small, manageable tasks. Fixing bugs, improving documentation, or working on minor features are great ways to familiarize yourself with the project. Starting small allows you to gain confidence and gradually take on more significant contributions.

   o **Tip**: Don't feel pressured to make huge changes right away. Starting with small contributions will help you learn how to interact with maintainers and understand the project's codebase before diving into bigger tasks.

3. **Understand the Contribution Guidelines**: Every open-source project has its own contribution guidelines, which dictate how to submit code, report issues, and interact with the community. It's essential to read and follow these guidelines carefully. By doing so, you ensure your contributions are aligned with the project's objectives and increase the likelihood of your pull requests being accepted.

o **Tip**: Familiarize yourself with the project's README file, code of conduct, and contribution documentation to understand the expected standards and procedures.

4. **Fork and Clone the Repository**: Once you've identified an issue or task to work on, fork the repository to your own GitHub account and clone it to your local machine. This allows you to make changes in your own copy of the project without affecting the main repository.

   o **Tip**: Use Git and GitHub to track your changes, and remember to sync your fork with the upstream repository to avoid conflicts.

5. **Submit a Pull Request (PR)**: After completing your changes, the next step is to submit a pull request. A PR is a way of submitting your contributions to the main repository for review. In the PR description, explain the changes you've made and why they are necessary.

   o **Tip**: When submitting your PR, be clear and detailed in your description. Provide context on what you've done and any relevant issue numbers. This makes it easier for maintainers to review and merge your code.

Why Open-Source Contributions Are Beneficial for Career Growth

1. **Skill Development**: Contributing to open-source projects is an excellent way to develop new technical skills and enhance your existing ones. Whether you're learning a new framework, working with databases, or improving your Git knowledge, open-source projects provide valuable hands-on experience.

   o **Example**: If you contribute to a project using a technology you're unfamiliar with (such as Kubernetes or GraphQL), you'll gain practical experience that is highly valuable in the job market.

2. **Networking and Collaboration**: Open-source contributions give you the opportunity to work with a global network of developers. Collaborating on projects and interacting with maintainers, other contributors, and reviewers helps you build relationships in the tech community. These

104

connections may lead to job offers, consulting opportunities, or even mentorship.

- o **Example**: Contributing to well-known open-source projects like React or TensorFlow can help you connect with developers who are influential in the tech community.

3. **Building a Reputation**: By contributing to open-source projects, you build a reputation as a reliable and skilled developer. Maintainers and other contributors will begin to recognize your work, and this can lead to more opportunities in the future.

- o **Example**: If your contributions to a popular project get merged and are consistently high quality, other developers may seek you out for collaborations or job opportunities.

4. **Demonstrating Initiative and Passion**: Employers and clients look for developers who take initiative and are passionate about their craft. Contributing to open-source projects shows that you care about software development beyond your own work and are dedicated to making the broader tech community better.

- Example: A developer who regularly contributes to open-source projects demonstrates their commitment to learning, collaboration, and continuous improvement—qualities that employers highly value.

Case Studies of Developers Who Grew Their Reputation by Contributing to Open-Source

1. **Dan   Abramov**

   Dan Abramov is the co-author of Redux and a well-known figure in the React ecosystem. His contributions to the React library and other open-source projects have earned him a strong reputation as a thought leader in front-end development. Dan has used open-source contributions as a stepping stone to broader recognition in the developer community, ultimately leading to a role at Facebook and opportunities to speak at conferences.

   - **Key Takeaway**: Dan's open-source work has positioned him as a leading figure in the JavaScript and React communities, showing how contributing to open-source can lead to career growth and industry recognition.

2. **Sarah**   **Drasner**

   Sarah Drasner, a prominent front-end developer and Vue.js core team member, has built her reputation through her contributions to the open-source community. Sarah not only contributes code but also writes detailed blog posts, gives talks, and participates in various open-source projects. Her visibility in the community has led to a strong personal brand as an expert in web animations and Vue.js development.

   - **Key Takeaway**: Sarah's contributions to both code and content creation have made her a leading voice in the front-end community, proving the power of combining open-source contributions with personal branding.

3. **Kent**   **C.**   **Dodds**

   Kent C. Dodds is a JavaScript expert and educator known for his contributions to open-source projects, including React and testing libraries. His work on open-source projects, combined with his educational content (courses, blog posts, and talks), has earned him recognition as a thought leader in the JavaScript and React communities.

o **Key Takeaway**: Kent's contributions to open-source, coupled with his focus on teaching and mentoring, have significantly raised his profile and positioned him as an influential figure in the web development world.

4. **TJ**   **Holowaychuk**

TJ Holowaychuk is a highly respected figure in the Node.js and JavaScript communities, known for his contributions to popular open-source projects such as Express.js and Koa. Through his work in the open-source community, TJ has built a strong personal brand and earned opportunities as a speaker and consultant.

o **Key Takeaway**: TJ's early contributions to critical projects in the Node.js ecosystem helped solidify his reputation as a leader and expert, showcasing how foundational open-source work can lead to long-term career growth.

Conclusion

Contributing to open-source projects is a powerful way to build your personal brand as a developer. It allows you to showcase your skills, collaborate with other developers, and increase your visibility within the community. Whether you're just starting out or looking to enhance your career, contributing to open-source is an invaluable step in your professional journey. By engaging with projects, writing meaningful code, and sharing your experiences, you not only improve your skills but also create a lasting impact on the broader tech community.

In the next chapter, we'll explore how networking and building relationships with other developers and industry professionals can further amplify your personal brand and career opportunities.

CHAPTER 10

NETWORKING FOR DEVELOPERS

How to Network Effectively Both Online and Offline

Networking is an essential part of building your personal brand as a developer. It's about building relationships that can lead to job opportunities, collaborations, mentorships, and partnerships. Networking helps you stay informed about industry trends, learn from others, and gain visibility in the developer community. Here's how to network effectively, both online and offline:

Online Networking

1. **Leverage Social Media**: Social media platforms like Twitter, LinkedIn, and GitHub provide excellent opportunities to engage with other developers, share knowledge, and learn from industry experts. Twitter, in particular, is widely used by developers to discuss industry trends, share resources, and participate in coding challenges.

    o **Tip**: Follow influencers, participate in relevant hashtags like #100DaysOfCode or #DevCommunity, and engage with others by commenting on posts and sharing your thoughts. Create a consistent presence to increase your visibility and attract like-minded professionals.

2. **Participate in Developer Communities**: Join online forums and communities where developers share ideas, discuss problems, and collaborate on projects. Platforms like Stack Overflow, Reddit (e.g., r/programming or r/webdev), Dev.to, and the GitHub Issues section of open-source projects are great places to engage with fellow developers.

    o **Tip**: Ask questions, provide answers, and contribute to discussions in a constructive manner. As you become more active, you'll gain credibility and be seen as a helpful member of the community.

3. **Blogging and Content Creation**: Writing blogs or creating content on platforms like Medium or Dev.to can help you connect with a wider audience and establish yourself as a thought leader.

Share your experiences, tutorials, or lessons learned to showcase your expertise and attract networking opportunities.

- o **Tip**: Engage with readers by responding to comments on your blog posts. This can lead to valuable connections and discussions with other developers who share similar interests.

4. **Engage on GitHub**: GitHub is not just for hosting code—it's also a community for developers. Contributing to open-source projects or starting your own repositories can help you connect with other developers who share your interests. You can collaborate on projects, learn from others, and get feedback on your code.

- o **Tip**: Participate in open-source issues or pull requests, and maintain an active profile with detailed READMEs and documentation. Interacting with repositories in your area of expertise can put you in touch with industry professionals and peers.

5. **Join Developer Slack Groups or Discord Servers**: Many tech communities host Slack groups or Discord servers where developers gather to discuss projects, seek advice, and network. These informal

environments are perfect for connecting with peers, asking questions, and even finding job opportunities.

- o **Tip**: Look for communities relevant to your interests (e.g., JavaScript, React, DevOps) and make a point to contribute. Ask questions, offer advice, and share your experiences.

Offline Networking

1. **Attend Meetups and Conferences**: Developer meetups, conferences, and workshops provide a great opportunity to meet people in person, learn new skills, and build relationships. Attending these events allows you to connect with people in your field and explore potential collaborations. It also gives you the chance to network with hiring managers, fellow developers, and potential clients.

   - o **Tip**: Attend events that focus on your niche (e.g., Python, machine learning, front-end development) to meet people with similar interests and expertise. Make sure to approach other attendees, exchange contact information, and follow up afterward to maintain the connection.

2. **Get Involved in Local Developer Communities**: Local meetups and community groups are an excellent way to network in person and create lasting relationships. Search for meetups in your area using platforms like Meetup.com or Eventbrite. These events often feature guest speakers, coding challenges, or hands-on workshops that provide great opportunities for networking.

   o **Tip**: Participate actively by volunteering to help organize events or by presenting a topic. This positions you as an engaged member of the community and allows you to meet other professionals who can become valuable contacts.

3. **Attend Hackathons and Coding Competitions**: Hackathons are great places to meet other developers, collaborate on projects, and compete in a fun and challenging environment. Whether it's a local or virtual hackathon, participating gives you the opportunity to work with others, showcase your skills, and potentially win prizes or recognition.

   o **Tip**: Use hackathons as an opportunity to meet potential collaborators or mentors. Even if you don't win, the experience and connections you make can lead to future opportunities.

4. **Join Industry Events and Talks**: Many tech conferences, product launches, and meetups offer sessions, talks, and workshops that focus on the latest industry trends. These events are excellent for learning new technologies, networking with industry leaders, and hearing from experts in your field.

   o **Tip**: Attend networking sessions during these events. Approach speakers after their talks, ask insightful questions, and introduce yourself to people who are actively involved in the tech scene.

5. **Volunteering**:

   Volunteering at tech conferences or local events is an excellent way to meet people while contributing to the community. You can network with other volunteers, speakers, and attendees while also giving back to the industry.

   o **Tip**: Offer to help with registration, event coordination, or speaker assistance. Volunteering positions you as a proactive member of the community and often leads to connections that wouldn't have happened otherwise.

Tips for Attending and Speaking at Conferences, Meetups, and Webinars

Networking is not just about meeting people—it's also about building meaningful relationships. Here are some tips for making the most out of attending and speaking at conferences, meetups, and webinars:

1. **Prepare Your Elevator Pitch**: When meeting people at conferences or meetups, have a concise elevator pitch ready. This should include who you are, what you do, and why you're passionate about it. Make it interesting and brief, leaving room for questions and follow-up.
   - **Tip**: Keep it engaging! Focus on what makes you unique and why you're attending the event.
2. **Ask Questions and Be Curious**: Networking is a two-way street. Asking insightful questions about the speaker's presentation or someone else's work shows that you're genuinely

interested in the conversation and not just looking for self-promotion.

   o **Tip**: After a talk or discussion, approach the speaker or attendees with a thoughtful question that demonstrates you've been paying attention and have something valuable to ask.

3. **Don't Be Afraid to Reach Out to Speakers or Influencers**:

   If you're attending a conference or webinar where industry leaders are speaking, don't hesitate to approach them afterward. Introduce yourself, mention something specific from their talk that you found insightful, and ask if they have any advice for someone in your position.

   o **Tip**: When you reach out to industry influencers, be polite and respectful of their time. Mention a specific aspect of their work that resonated with you, and express genuine interest in their journey or advice.

4. **Engage During Q&A Sessions**:
   During conferences, meetups, or webinars, engaging in Q&A sessions is a great way to get noticed. If you have a relevant, thought-provoking question, don't

be afraid to ask it during the session. It can be an excellent opportunity to network with speakers and attendees.

- o **Tip**: Be prepared with a question that adds value to the discussion. Avoid asking questions that can easily be answered through a quick search.

5. **Follow** **Up**: After meeting people at an event, follow up with them to maintain the connection. Send a brief email or LinkedIn message thanking them for the conversation, referencing something specific from your interaction, and expressing interest in staying in touch.

- o **Tip**: Keep your follow-up emails concise and personal. Mention something specific about the event or conversation to jog their memory and make the message feel genuine.

How to Connect with Industry Influencers and Peers

Connecting with industry influencers and peers is a crucial part of expanding your network and building your personal brand. Here are some effective ways to do so:

1. **Be Active on Social Media**: Industry influencers often engage with their followers on Twitter, LinkedIn, and other platforms. Participate in conversations, comment on their posts, and share your thoughts on the topics they discuss.

   o **Tip**: Don't just passively follow them—engage with their content by sharing your own insights, asking questions, or offering helpful resources.

2. **Collaborate on Projects**: One of the best ways to form connections with peers and influencers is by collaborating on projects. Reach out to developers who share similar interests and propose a collaboration, whether it's working on an open-source project, writing a blog post together, or hosting a webinar.

   o **Tip**: Make sure you're offering something valuable in the collaboration. It's not just about what you can gain but about how you can contribute to the other person's goals as well.

3. **Attend and Participate in Industry Events**: Networking doesn't stop once you've met an influencer or peer. Attend their webinars, comment

119

on their blog posts, or participate in their projects to maintain the relationship and further engage with their work.

- o **Tip**: Continue to interact with the people you meet at events, even after the event ends. This long-term engagement helps to solidify connections and build stronger professional relationships.

Conclusion

Networking is a vital aspect of growing your personal brand as a developer. By actively engaging both online and offline, attending conferences, contributing to discussions, and connecting with influencers and peers, you can build a robust professional network that opens up new opportunities for collaboration, mentorship, and career growth.

In the next chapter, we will explore how to manage your career growth and track your progress as you continue to build your personal brand.

CHAPTER 11

LEVERAGING SOCIAL MEDIA FOR YOUR BRAND

How to Use Twitter, GitHub, and Other Platforms to Share Knowledge

In today's digital age, social media platforms are essential tools for developers to share knowledge, connect with peers, and build a personal brand. Platforms like Twitter, GitHub, LinkedIn, and Stack Overflow provide developers with the opportunity to showcase their skills, engage with industry leaders, and grow a professional network. Here's how you can use these platforms to effectively share knowledge and build your brand:

1. Twitter

Twitter is a popular platform for developers to share insights, participate in discussions, and engage with the broader tech community. It's a fast-paced, real-time platform where you can stay up to date with the latest trends and contribute your own thoughts.

- **Share Knowledge and Resources**: Regularly share valuable resources, links to articles, tutorials, or coding challenges that your audience will find useful. You can also retweet insightful posts from other developers to engage with the community.

  - **Example**: A developer could tweet about a new framework they've been experimenting with, sharing key takeaways or challenges faced during their experience, along with a helpful resource link.

- **Engage with Hashtags**: Participate in developer-specific hashtags such as #100DaysOfCode, #DevCommunity, or #WebDev. These hashtags connect you with other developers and create opportunities for conversation and collaboration.

  - **Example**: If you're working on a React project, you could use hashtags like #ReactJS or #FrontendDevelopment to increase the visibility of your posts and reach a targeted audience interested in those topics.

- **Join Developer Discussions**: Twitter is home to many tech discussions. Join conversations about new technologies, industry trends, or even popular coding challenges. By actively contributing, you can establish yourself as an engaged member of the community.

- o **Tip**: When joining discussions, add value by offering insights or asking thoughtful questions. Being active in trending tech conversations will increase your visibility.

2. GitHub

GitHub is the go-to platform for hosting code and collaborating on open-source projects. It's a great way to demonstrate your skills, share projects, and interact with other developers. Here's how to leverage GitHub:

- **Share Your Projects**: Posting your own projects on GitHub allows you to showcase your work and provide a portfolio of your coding skills. Ensure your repositories are well-documented with clear README files and include examples of what the project does.
  - o **Example**: If you've developed a weather app or a machine learning algorithm, share the code on GitHub with clear instructions on

how to use or contribute. This can attract other developers who may want to collaborate or give you feedback.

- **Contribute to Open-Source**: Participating in open-source projects is an excellent way to demonstrate your expertise. By contributing to popular repositories, you not only show your coding skills but also engage with a global community of developers.

  o **Tip**: Focus on projects that align with your skills or areas of interest. Your contributions can get noticed by project maintainers and other developers, which helps expand your professional network.

- **Showcase Your Knowledge with GitHub Pages**: GitHub Pages allows you to host a website or documentation for free. You can use it to create a personal site or portfolio, or even blog about your development journey. This acts as an extension of your GitHub profile, providing more opportunities for people to find your work.

  o **Example**: You could host a personal portfolio or a technical blog about specific projects, challenges you've faced, and the solutions you implemented, helping others learn from your experience.

3. LinkedIn

LinkedIn is a professional networking platform where you can connect with colleagues, recruiters, potential clients, and other industry professionals. Here's how you can leverage LinkedIn for your brand:

- **Share Articles and Updates**: Use LinkedIn's status update feature to share articles, thoughts on industry trends, or updates on your projects. Posting regularly helps keep you visible to your network and shows that you are actively engaged in the tech community.
    - o **Tip**: Share your blog posts, open-source contributions, or relevant industry news. Engage with your network by commenting on others' posts or starting discussions around emerging technologies.
- **Join LinkedIn Groups**: LinkedIn has many professional groups where developers share knowledge, discuss trends, and seek advice. Joining and actively participating in

125

relevant groups can increase your credibility and allow you to network with like-minded professionals.

- o **Example**: You could join a group dedicated to React developers or machine learning and participate by answering questions or sharing relevant resources.

4. Stack Overflow

Stack Overflow is a popular platform for developers to ask technical questions, share knowledge, and collaborate with others. It's an excellent way to demonstrate your expertise and help others while learning in the process.

- **Answer Questions and Provide Solutions**: By answering questions related to your expertise, you help others while showcasing your problem-solving skills. Giving well-thought-out, high-quality answers can build your reputation on the platform, making you a trusted contributor in your field.
  - o **Tip**: Start by answering questions that align with your skills. As you gain more experience and recognition, you'll start

getting more upvotes and visibility within the community.

- **Ask Thoughtful Questions**: Don't hesitate to ask questions, especially when you're stuck on a problem. Asking insightful questions and interacting with others' answers is an excellent way to learn, grow your network, and engage in technical discussions.

  - o **Tip**: When asking a question, make sure it's well-written and clear, with all the necessary context. This increases your chances of getting detailed, helpful answers.

Crafting Posts That Highlight Your Expertise and Attract Followers

Once you understand how to use social media platforms effectively, it's important to craft posts that highlight your expertise and attract followers. Here are some tips for creating engaging and valuable content:

1. **Be Consistent and Authentic**: Consistency is key to building an online presence. Post regularly about topics that interest you and align with your expertise. It's also important to be

authentic—let your personality shine through your posts. People are more likely to engage with you if they feel a personal connection.

- o **Tip**: Establish a posting schedule to stay consistent, whether it's daily, weekly, or bi-weekly.

2. **Share Your Journey**: Don't just share your successes—share your challenges and learning moments. Posting about how you overcame a specific bug or solved a problem can resonate with others and show that you're a real, relatable person.

- o **Example**: "I spent hours debugging this issue with my React app. Here's what I learned about state management that could save you time."

3. **Use Visuals and Code Snippets**: People are more likely to engage with content that includes visuals, such as images, infographics, or videos. Code snippets are also highly effective on platforms like Twitter and LinkedIn, especially if you're explaining a technical solution.

- o **Tip**: When sharing code on Twitter or GitHub, make sure it's well-formatted and easy to understand. Use screenshots or screen recordings when explaining complex concepts.

4. **Ask Questions and Encourage Engagement**: Posts that ask questions or encourage discussions tend to get more engagement. By creating content that invites others to share their thoughts, you increase the chances of interaction, which can lead to more followers.

   o **Example**: "What's your go-to strategy for optimizing front-end performance in React? Share your tips below!"

5. **Collaborate and Cross-Promote**: Collaborating with other developers or sharing others' content is a great way to build relationships and expand your reach. Cross-promoting with other developers can introduce you to new audiences and help you grow your network.

   o **Tip**: Reach out to other developers whose work you admire and see if you can collaborate on a post, project, or talk.

Real Examples of Developers Who Have Built Large Followings Through Social Media

1. **Kent C. Dodds**

   Kent C. Dodds, a well-known React educator, built his large following by consistently sharing educational content on Twitter and writing technical blog posts. His willingness to engage with the community and share his personal learning journey has made him a go-to resource for React developers.

   o **Key Takeaway**: Kent's content is consistently educational, helpful, and accessible. He's known for his approachable style and willingness to teach, which has attracted a loyal following of learners and developers.

2. **Sarah Drasner**

   Sarah Drasner is a front-end developer and Vue.js core team member who has built a significant following through her blog, conference talks, and social media presence. Sarah shares tutorials, thoughts on web development trends, and personal insights about her development journey, helping others in the community while building her brand.

130

- o **Key Takeaway**: Sarah engages with her audience through multiple platforms—Twitter, GitHub, and her blog—creating a well-rounded, visible personal brand. Her authenticity and willingness to help others have made her one of the most respected voices in the front-end community.

3. **Mosh   Hamedani**

   Mosh Hamedani, a software engineer and educator, has built a large following by creating and sharing high-quality educational content on YouTube and social media. His posts and tutorials focus on topics like C#, React, and Node.js, attracting both beginner and advanced developers looking to improve their skills.

   - o **Key Takeaway**: Mosh's success comes from consistently delivering valuable, easy-to-follow tutorials and engaging with his audience. His willingness to teach and mentor has positioned him as a leader in the development community.

4. **Chris   Coyier**

   Chris Coyier, the creator of CSS-Tricks and co-founder of CodePen, has built his following by consistently creating valuable web development content. His blog posts, tutorials, and Twitter presence have made him a well-known figure in the front-end development world.

- o **Key Takeaway**: Chris's content is relatable and useful, focusing on practical web development solutions. His engagement with the community through blog posts, forums, and social media has helped him build a large and loyal following.

Conclusion

Leveraging social media platforms like Twitter, GitHub, and LinkedIn is essential for developers looking to build their personal brand and grow their career opportunities. By consistently sharing knowledge, engaging with the community, and showcasing your expertise, you can attract a larger following and position yourself as an authority in your niche. Social media is a powerful tool to network, learn, and connect with others, but it's important to stay authentic and add value to the conversations happening around you.

In the next chapter, we will explore how to further build and maintain relationships with other developers, mentors, and industry leaders to help amplify your personal brand and career growth.

CHAPTER 12

MASTERING THE ART OF PUBLIC SPEAKING

Why Public Speaking Can Be a Powerful Tool for Your Personal Brand

Public speaking is one of the most effective ways to establish yourself as an authority in your field, increase your visibility, and share your expertise with a broader audience. As a developer, speaking at conferences, webinars, or meetups can provide immense benefits to your personal brand. Here's why public speaking is such a powerful tool:

1. **Establishes Authority and Thought Leadership**: Speaking at events positions you as an expert in your field. When you share your knowledge, experiences, and solutions to common problems, you build trust and credibility. Public speaking allows you to show that you not only have the skills but also the ability to teach and inspire others.

    o **Example**: A developer who speaks about advanced React techniques or shares their experience building scalable applications demonstrates deep expertise, making them a go-to resource for others in the tech community.

2. **Expands Your Reach and Audience**: Public speaking allows you to reach a wider audience than you could through online content alone. Whether you're speaking at a conference with hundreds of attendees or hosting a webinar for a global audience, you can share your insights with people from different parts of the world. This expands your network and helps you build relationships with people who might otherwise never come across your work.

   o **Example**: Speaking at a major tech conference or hosting a webinar on an emerging technology can introduce you to a new audience of developers, potential clients, or collaborators who may be interested in your work.

3. **Enhances Networking Opportunities**: Public speaking creates networking opportunities that are often not possible through online engagement alone. After your talk or session, you'll have the chance to meet fellow speakers, attendees,

and industry leaders. These interactions can lead to new job offers, collaborations, and even partnerships, all of which can help propel your career forward.

- o **Example**: A developer who speaks about their experience contributing to an open-source project might meet other contributors or project maintainers who could offer them collaborative opportunities or job leads.

4. **Boosts Confidence and Communication Skills**: Public speaking hones your ability to communicate clearly and confidently, which is a valuable skill for any developer. Whether you're explaining technical concepts to a non-technical audience or discussing new technologies with other experts, speaking in front of others improves your overall communication abilities.

- o **Example**: Giving a presentation on how you solved a particular coding challenge helps you develop the skill of articulating complex technical concepts in a way that anyone can understand, boosting both your confidence and your ability to explain your work to clients or colleagues.

5. **Creates Long-Lasting Impact**: Talks, webinars, and presentations can be recorded and shared widely, creating long-lasting content that serves as a reference for others in the future. These materials can continue to enhance your personal brand long after the event has ended, making it a valuable investment of your time.

   o **Example**: A well-recorded conference talk on JavaScript frameworks can be uploaded to YouTube or other platforms, continuing to attract viewers and expanding your reach for years to come.

How to Get Started with Speaking at Conferences or Hosting Webinars

If you're new to public speaking, the idea of standing in front of a large audience might feel daunting. However, with the right approach, you can start small and gradually build your confidence and speaking experience. Here's how you can get started with speaking at conferences or hosting webinars:

1. Start Small with Meetups and Local Events

Before jumping into large conferences or webinars, start by speaking at local meetups, coding workshops, or small community events. These smaller audiences provide a low-pressure environment where you can practice your speaking skills and gain experience.

- **Tip**: Look for meetups or user groups related to your area of expertise (e.g., JavaScript, Python, web development). These events often welcome speakers who are willing to share their knowledge.
- **Example**: If you're passionate about a specific technology or framework, you can offer to give a talk at a local meetup. These smaller events are a great starting point to test the waters and refine your speaking style.

2. Develop Your Speaking Topics

Choose topics that you're passionate about and knowledgeable in. Topics should align with your personal brand and target audience, providing value to the listeners while highlighting your expertise. Think about the kinds of challenges you've faced, the solutions you've implemented, and the lessons you've learned—these can serve as the foundation for great talks.

- **Tip**: Focus on solving common problems or providing insights into emerging technologies that others might be struggling with. This approach ensures that your talk will resonate with the audience.
- **Example**: A developer with experience building scalable web applications might give a talk on "Optimizing React Performance for Large-Scale Applications," which addresses a common concern among developers.

3. Submit Speaking Proposals to Conferences

Once you're comfortable speaking at smaller events, start submitting proposals to larger conferences. Many conferences have open call-for-papers (CFP) sessions where you can submit your topics and abstracts. Look for tech conferences related to your area of expertise, and craft a well-written proposal that clearly explains the value of your talk.

- **Tip**: Focus on clear, actionable takeaways in your proposal. Organizers are more likely to accept talks that promise to teach attendees something they can apply immediately.
- **Example**: Submit a proposal to a React or JavaScript conference with a detailed outline of your session, including the goals, structure, and expected learning outcomes.

4. Host Webinars or Online Workshops

If you prefer a more controlled, interactive environment, consider hosting webinars or online workshops. Webinars allow you to engage with an audience remotely, making them a great option if you're not yet ready for large live audiences. Platforms like Zoom, YouTube Live, or even GitHub Live are perfect for hosting technical webinars.

- **Tip**: Plan your webinar to be interactive. Encourage attendees to ask questions and engage with you during the session. This makes the experience more memorable and educational.
- **Example**: Host a webinar where you walk through building a simple app with a new framework or demonstrate how to debug complex issues in a

codebase. Offer participants a chance to ask questions or share their own experiences.

5. Practice and Refine Your Presentation Skills

Preparation is key to a successful presentation. Practice your talk in front of friends, family, or colleagues, and ask for feedback. Make sure your presentation is engaging, well-paced, and visually appealing. Use slides or demos to illustrate key points, and avoid information overload.

- **Tip**: Record your practice sessions and review them. This can help you identify areas where you can improve, whether it's pacing, tone, or clarity.
- **Example**: Use tools like PowerPoint or Google Slides to create visually engaging presentations. Make sure to avoid overcrowding slides with too much text—use bullet points and visuals to keep the audience engaged.

Success Stories of Developers Who Have Used Public Speaking to Elevate Their Careers

Public speaking has helped many developers establish their personal brands, gain recognition in their fields, and open new career opportunities. Here are a few examples of

141

developers who have used public speaking to elevate their careers:

1. **Dan** **Abramov**

   Dan Abramov, co-creator of Redux and a key figure in the React community, built a strong personal brand through his blog, talks, and conference presentations. By speaking at various JavaScript conferences and contributing to online discussions, Dan became one of the most influential figures in front-end development.

   - **Key Takeaway**: Dan's ability to simplify complex React concepts and share them with the community through talks has established him as a thought leader, earning him widespread recognition and opportunities to work at Facebook.

2. **Sarah** **Drasner**

   Sarah Drasner, a front-end developer and Vue.js core team member, used public speaking as a way to build her brand and expand her influence. Her talks at major tech conferences and workshops on web animation, SVG, and front-end development have made her a prominent voice in the tech community.

- o **Key Takeaway**: Sarah's focus on web animation and her ability to explain complex topics in an approachable way have helped her gain a large following. Her public speaking career allowed her to share her passion for development and establish herself as a thought leader in front-end development.

3. **Kent C. Dodds**

Kent C. Dodds, a JavaScript educator and advocate for testing, has used public speaking as a way to spread his message about best practices in software development. His talks on testing and JavaScript have made him a sought-after speaker at conferences, and his teaching work, including online courses and workshops, has significantly boosted his personal brand.

- o **Key Takeaway**: Kent's focus on teaching developers how to improve their skills through testing and best practices has resonated with a large audience. His speaking career has opened doors for him to create educational content and further establish his influence in the developer community.

4. **Mosh**   **Hamedani**

Mosh Hamedani, an educator and software engineer, built his personal brand by speaking at conferences and creating educational content through his blog, YouTube, and online courses. He used his speaking engagements to teach developers about modern web development technologies, including React, Node.js, and .NET.

- o **Key Takeaway**: Mosh's ability to break down complex topics and engage audiences has made him one of the leading educators in software development. His speaking career has led to a strong online presence and the opportunity to create his own educational courses.

Conclusion

Mastering the art of public speaking is a powerful way to elevate your personal brand as a developer. Whether you're speaking at conferences, hosting webinars, or sharing your knowledge at local meetups, public speaking helps establish your authority, expand your reach, and create lasting connections in the tech community. By starting small, preparing thoroughly, and focusing on providing value to your audience, you can use public speaking to open new career opportunities and build a stronger professional presence.

In the next chapter, we will explore how to develop and execute your career strategy, ensuring long-term growth and success as you continue to build your personal brand.

CHAPTER 13

BUILDING A YOUTUBE OR STREAMING PRESENCE

The Power of Video Content for Developers

In today's digital world, video content is one of the most effective ways to engage with your audience and build a personal brand. As a developer, using video platforms like YouTube or streaming services like Twitch can significantly boost your visibility, credibility, and reach. Here's why video content is so powerful for developers:

1. **Engagement and Reach**: Video content is more engaging than written content alone. Viewers are more likely to stay focused and connect with your personality, ideas, and communication style when they see you in action. With the rise of platforms like YouTube, millions of people are actively searching for coding tutorials, problem-solving videos, and tech-related content, making video an ideal medium for reaching a broader audience.

o **Example**: Viewers who watch a tutorial video are more likely to follow you or share your content because they've been able to engage with you in a personal and dynamic way. This can lead to more followers, potential job opportunities, and collaboration offers.

2. **Visual Learning and Demonstration**: Developers often face challenges that are easier to understand when they can see the code in action. Video allows you to showcase complex concepts or demonstrate code in a way that written content simply can't. Live coding sessions or tutorials let viewers follow along with real examples, making the learning process more interactive and impactful.

o **Example**: If you're explaining how to build a to-do list app using React, showing the code in real-time as you walk through the process helps the viewer better understand the logic and structure of the code.

3. **Building Trust and Authenticity**: Video allows you to connect with your audience on a more personal level. They can see your facial expressions, hear your tone of voice, and get a sense

of your passion and enthusiasm for the subject matter. This human connection can foster trust and loyalty among your viewers, which is essential for building a personal brand.

- o **Example**: Developers who are authentic and personable on camera can gain a following of viewers who trust their advice, making them more likely to engage with their content and follow their recommendations.

4. **Increased Discoverability and SEO Benefits**: Video content, especially on platforms like YouTube, offers a significant SEO advantage. YouTube is the second-largest search engine in the world, and your videos can appear in search results, giving you the chance to reach a larger audience. Properly optimized titles, descriptions, and tags can help your videos rank higher, leading to more views and subscribers.

- o **Tip**: Use keywords that are relevant to your topic, such as "JavaScript tutorial," "React JS course," or "how to build a website," to improve the chances of your videos being discovered by people searching for those terms.

Setting Up a YouTube or Streaming Channel to Share Tutorials, Talks, or Live Coding Sessions

Building a YouTube or streaming presence requires more than just creating content—it's about creating a channel that represents your brand and engages your audience. Here's how to set up your channel for success:

1. Choosing the Right Platform

While YouTube is the most popular video-sharing platform, there are other platforms you can consider, such as Twitch, GitHub Live, or even Vimeo for niche audiences. The platform you choose should align with your content style and your target audience.

- **YouTube**: Best for creating tutorials, tech talks, educational content, and long-form videos. It's a powerful search engine with massive reach.
- **Twitch**: Ideal for live streaming, especially if you want to interact with your audience in real time. It's a popular platform for developers who want to stream coding sessions or live builds.
- **GitHub Live**: A newer option that allows you to stream and record content related to coding and

software development directly within the GitHub ecosystem. It's a good platform for more technical, community-focused content.

2. Setting Up Your Channel

Setting up your channel involves creating a user-friendly and professional appearance that aligns with your personal brand. Here are some key elements to focus on:

- **Create a Professional Branding**: Your channel name, logo, banner, and tagline should be consistent with your personal brand. Choose a channel name that reflects your niche or specialty (e.g., "CodeWithMosh" or "JavaScriptMastery").
  - **Tip**: Design a clean and recognizable logo and banner. Tools like Canva or Adobe Spark offer free templates to help you create professional designs.
- **Craft an Engaging Channel Description**: Your channel description should be clear and concise, explaining who you are, what kind of content you produce, and why people should subscribe. This is the first thing new viewers will read, so make it compelling.

150

- o **Example**: "Welcome to [Your Channel Name], where I teach you how to build web apps, master coding techniques, and stay ahead in the tech industry. Whether you're a beginner or an experienced developer, my tutorials will help you level up your skills."

- **Customize Your Channel Layout**: Organize your videos into playlists based on themes or topics. This makes it easier for new viewers to find content relevant to their interests and improves the user experience.

  - o **Example**: Create playlists like "React Tutorials for Beginners," "JavaScript Fundamentals," or "Web Development Tips and Tricks" to organize your content.

3. Creating High-Quality Content

To build a following, you need to create engaging, valuable, and informative content. Here's how you can do that:

- **Tutorials**:
  Create step-by-step tutorials that teach specific skills or concepts. Make sure your tutorials are easy to follow, with clear explanations, code examples, and

actionable takeaways. This is one of the most popular types of content for developers.

- **Example**: "How to Build a Todo App with React" or "Mastering CSS Grid in 30 Minutes."

- **Live Coding Sessions**: Live coding allows you to work on a project in real-time, answering questions from viewers and showing your problem-solving process. These sessions are a great way to engage with your audience and show your coding workflow.

  - **Tip**: Use a platform like Twitch or YouTube Live for streaming. Engage with viewers by answering questions in the chat and explaining your thought process as you code.

- **Tech Talks and Reviews**: Share your insights on new technologies, libraries, or frameworks. You can do deep dives into new tools or provide opinions on trends in the industry.

  - **Example**: "React vs. Vue: Which is Better for Web Development?" or "A Beginner's Guide to Serverless Architecture."

4. Engage and Interact with Your Audience

Building a community is key to growing your channel. Encourage viewers to comment, ask questions, and provide feedback. Respond to comments and interact with your audience on social media to keep the conversation going beyond the video.

- **Tip**: Include a call-to-action in your videos, encouraging viewers to like, comment, and subscribe. Ask open-ended questions in your videos to stimulate engagement.
- **Example**: "What features would you like to see in future tutorials? Leave your thoughts in the comments below!"

5. Consistency and Scheduling

Consistency is critical to growing your YouTube or streaming presence. Uploading regularly helps keep your audience engaged and encourages them to return for more content.

- **Tip**: Create a content calendar and stick to a regular posting schedule, whether that's weekly, bi-weekly, or monthly. Let your viewers know when to expect new content.

- **Example**: "New coding tutorials every Friday at 12 PM."

Examples of Developers Who Have Successfully Built an Audience via YouTube

1. **Mosh Hamedani (CodeWithMosh)** Mosh Hamedani is a well-known software engineer and educator who has built a large following on YouTube by providing high-quality, beginner-friendly tutorials on technologies like React, Node.js, and C#. His channel, "CodeWithMosh," has over 1 million subscribers, and he has successfully turned his YouTube presence into a full-fledged educational business, offering online courses and tutorials.

   o **Key Takeaway**: Mosh's success lies in his ability to break down complex topics into digestible, easy-to-understand content. His consistency in posting valuable tutorials has built a loyal and engaged audience.

2. **Traversy Media (Brad Traversy)** Brad Traversy's channel, "Traversy Media," is one of the most popular YouTube channels for web

development tutorials. He covers a wide range of topics, from basic HTML/CSS to advanced JavaScript frameworks like React and Node.js. With over 1 million subscribers, Brad has successfully used YouTube to build a personal brand as a web development educator.

- o **Key Takeaway**: Brad's channel is successful because of the diversity of content, high production value, and approachable teaching style. His practical tutorials make complex topics easy to understand.

3. **The Coding Train (Daniel Shiffman)**
   Daniel Shiffman's channel, "The Coding Train," is known for its engaging and fun coding tutorials. He specializes in creative coding, teaching topics such as p5.js, Processing, and machine learning. Daniel's personality and enthusiasm are key to his success, and he's built a strong community of learners and collaborators.

- o **Key Takeaway**: Daniel's unique approach to teaching—combining creativity with coding—has made him stand out in the tech education space. His enthusiasm and

155

approachable style have created a loyal following.

4. **Fireship   (Jeff   Delaney)**

Jeff Delaney's channel, "Fireship," provides quick and high-quality videos on modern web development topics, including Firebase, React, and cloud computing. He has built a significant following by focusing on short, concise tutorials that get straight to the point.

o **Key Takeaway**: Jeff's success comes from his ability to deliver concise, no-fluff content that is both educational and entertaining. His "100 Seconds of Code" series, which provides quick insights into different topics, has helped him build a broad audience.

Conclusion

Building a YouTube or streaming presence can significantly boost your personal brand as a developer. By creating valuable, high-quality video content, you can engage with a broader audience, showcase your expertise, and establish yourself as a thought leader in your field. Whether you're sharing tutorials, hosting live coding sessions, or offering technical talks, video content is a powerful tool for building your brand and advancing your career.

In the next chapter, we will discuss how to effectively monetize your personal brand as a developer, turning your skills and online presence into sustainable income streams.

CHAPTER 14

PUBLISHING A BOOK OR EBOOK

How Writing a Book Can Enhance Your Credibility as an Expert

Writing a book, whether it's a traditional print book or an eBook, is one of the most powerful ways to solidify your authority and enhance your credibility as an expert in your field. As a developer, publishing a book can set you apart from your peers and establish you as a thought leader in the tech community. Here's how writing a book can elevate your personal brand:

1. **Showcases Deep Knowledge**: Writing a book requires an in-depth understanding of your subject matter. By going through the process of writing, researching, and compiling your thoughts, you demonstrate not only your technical expertise but also your ability to communicate complex topics clearly and effectively. This gives readers the confidence that you are a true authority in your area of focus.

o **Example**: A developer who writes a book on machine learning will position themselves as an expert in the field, especially if the book covers advanced topics or provides innovative approaches to solving real-world problems.

2. **Builds Trust and Credibility**: A published book is a tangible demonstration of your expertise. It provides a permanent, verifiable reference to your knowledge and experience. When potential clients, employers, or collaborators see that you've written a book, they are more likely to trust your skills and judgment.

o **Example**: A developer who has written a comprehensive guide to building scalable cloud applications will be seen as a reliable source of information on cloud computing and may be sought after for consulting or speaking opportunities.

3. **Reaches a Wider Audience**: While blogging and creating videos allow you to reach an audience, a book can have a much broader reach. Books are often distributed globally and can be found by anyone searching for solutions or

educational content in your niche. They are also considered more formal and respected than shorter-form content, which adds to your credibility.

- o **Example**: Publishing a book on a popular platform like Amazon can expose your work to a global audience, from beginners to experienced professionals, who are eager to learn from your expertise.

4. **Increases Opportunities for Speaking Engagements**:

   Authors are often invited to speak at conferences, webinars, and meetups. Having a published book gives you a platform to pitch yourself as a speaker and offers you the opportunity to present your ideas and insights in front of a live audience. This increases your visibility and creates more networking opportunities.

   - o **Example**: Authors who have written books about React or JavaScript are frequently invited to speak at tech conferences, where they can further establish their reputation and share their knowledge in person.

Tips on Publishing, Marketing, and Distributing Technical Books

Publishing a book involves more than just writing it—it requires careful planning, marketing, and distribution to ensure that your work reaches the right audience and has the impact you desire. Here are some tips for successfully publishing and promoting your technical book:

1. Decide Between Traditional and Self-Publishing

There are two main routes to publishing: traditional publishing and self-publishing. Each has its pros and cons, so choose the one that aligns with your goals.

- **Traditional Publishing**: Traditional publishers offer the benefit of professional editing, design, and marketing, as well as access to established distribution channels. However, this route often requires securing a literary agent, and it can take longer to get your book published.
  - o **Tip**: If you choose traditional publishing, research publishers in your niche (e.g., tech publishers) and submit a compelling proposal

to showcase your expertise and the value of your book to the market.

- **Self-Publishing**:

Self-publishing allows you to maintain full control over the content, design, and marketing of your book. Platforms like Amazon Kindle Direct Publishing (KDP) make it easy to publish and distribute your book to a global audience. However, you will be responsible for everything, including editing, marketing, and distribution.

  - **Tip**: Self-publishing platforms like KDP, Smashwords, and Lulu make the process simpler. Be sure to invest in professional editing and cover design to ensure your book is polished and visually appealing.

2. Focus on a Niche Topic

When writing a technical book, it's important to focus on a specific niche. General topics are harder to market and may not attract the right audience. Instead, select a specialized area within your field that addresses common challenges or needs.

- **Example**: Instead of writing a broad book on programming, consider a niche topic such as "Advanced JavaScript Patterns," "Mastering Kubernetes for Developers," or "The Complete Guide to Building Scalable APIs."
- **Tip**: Research existing books in your field and identify gaps where your expertise can offer new insights or solutions. This will help you position your book in a unique and valuable way.

3. Marketing and Promotion Strategies

Once your book is written and published, marketing is crucial to ensure it reaches your intended audience. Here are some strategies to effectively promote your technical book:

- **Leverage Your Existing Network**: Start by promoting your book to your existing network of followers, social media connections, colleagues, and industry peers. Ask for reviews, share the book in relevant forums, and encourage others to spread the word.
  - o **Tip**: Announce your book on platforms like Twitter, LinkedIn, and GitHub. Create posts,

blog about it, and offer sneak peeks or sample chapters to generate interest.

- **Use Your Website and Blog**: If you have a personal website or blog, use it as a platform to promote your book. Create dedicated pages for your book, share your writing journey, and offer a downloadable PDF excerpt or an early-bird discount to generate initial sales.
  - o **Tip**: Include call-to-action buttons and links on your website, directing visitors to the book's sales page on Amazon or your self-publishing platform.
- **Offer Discounts or Bundle Deals**: Consider offering discounts or bundle deals to encourage early purchases. This is particularly useful when launching your book, as it can generate momentum and initial reviews that will help increase visibility.
  - o **Tip**: Offer a limited-time discount or bundle the book with additional resources like a video course or exclusive access to a webinar.
- **Engage in Guest Blogging and Podcast Interviews**: Contributing guest blog posts or participating in

podcast interviews related to your book's topic can increase exposure and drive traffic to your book. Being featured on popular industry blogs and podcasts helps you reach an audience interested in your expertise.

- o **Tip**: Reach out to influencers in your niche and offer to write guest posts or be interviewed about your book and its contents.

- **Collect Reviews and Testimonials**: Encourage readers to leave reviews on Amazon, Goodreads, or other platforms. Positive reviews help boost credibility and attract more readers. You can also showcase testimonials on your website or in your marketing materials.

  - o **Tip**: Provide advanced readers (beta readers) with a free copy in exchange for their honest reviews. Share these reviews on your social media or website to build trust with potential buyers.

4. Distribution Channels

Your book's distribution strategy is just as important as the writing itself. Here are a few key distribution options:

- **Amazon Kindle Direct Publishing (KDP)**: Amazon KDP is one of the most popular self-publishing platforms. It allows you to publish eBooks and print books and distribute them globally. Amazon also offers tools to track sales, manage pricing, and take advantage of Kindle Unlimited for wider exposure.
    - o **Tip**: Use KDP Select to make your book available for free or at a discounted rate for a limited time. This strategy can help generate reviews and boost sales in the long run.
- **Smashwords**:
  Smashwords is another great self-publishing platform that allows you to distribute eBooks to a variety of retailers, including Barnes & Noble, Kobo, and Apple Books.
    - o **Tip**: Distribute your book on multiple platforms to maximize your reach, but ensure that your marketing efforts align with the distribution channels you use.
- **Print-on-Demand (POD) Services**: If you want to offer a physical copy of your book, use print-on-demand services such as Lulu, Blurb, or IngramSpark. These platforms print your book as

orders come in, saving you the cost of maintaining an inventory.

- o **Tip**: Offer both digital and print versions of your book to cater to different reader preferences.

Stories of Developers Who Gained Recognition by Writing Books

1. **Kyle Simpson (You Don't Know JS)** Kyle Simpson, a well-known JavaScript developer and educator, gained significant recognition through his book series, "You Don't Know JS." The series dives deep into JavaScript, covering topics that are often overlooked in mainstream tutorials. The books have been widely praised for their thoroughness and clarity, establishing Kyle as an authority on JavaScript.

   - o **Key Takeaway**: Kyle's ability to take a niche subject (advanced JavaScript concepts) and write a series of comprehensive, well-structured books helped him build a reputation as one of the leading JavaScript experts in the world.

2. **Mosh Hamedani (The Complete Guide to Modern JavaScript)**

Mosh Hamedani, a popular YouTube educator and software engineer, expanded his personal brand by writing books on JavaScript and web development. His book "The Complete Guide to Modern JavaScript" has helped countless developers learn JavaScript, and his success with books has been complemented by his video courses.

  o **Key Takeaway**: Mosh's consistent content creation, both in books and video formats, has positioned him as a trusted resource for developers. His books serve as a natural extension of his teaching style, providing additional depth to his lessons.

3. **Scott Hanselman (The ASP.NET Developer's Cookbook)**

Scott Hanselman, a prominent figure in the .NET and Microsoft development communities, gained recognition through his books and technical content. His book, "The ASP.NET Developer's Cookbook," has been a go-to resource for developers working with ASP.NET technologies, and his personal blog and podcast have further amplified his reach.

- o **Key Takeaway**: Scott's ability to break down complex technical content into digestible formats has made him a respected figure in the development community. His book is an example of how technical writing can help cement your position as an expert.

Conclusion

Writing a book or eBook can dramatically enhance your personal brand as a developer. It establishes you as an expert in your field, builds trust with your audience, and opens doors for speaking opportunities and collaborations. Whether you choose to self-publish or go the traditional route, the key to success is choosing a niche topic, creating high-quality content, and marketing your book effectively.

In the next chapter, we will explore strategies for monetizing your personal brand and turning your expertise into multiple streams of income.

CHAPTER 15

ENGAGING WITH DEVELOPER COMMUNITIES

Why Active Participation in Developer Communities Matters

Engaging with developer communities is a vital aspect of building your personal brand and establishing yourself as a respected figure in the tech industry. Active participation in these communities can help you grow your network, gain visibility, and build credibility among your peers. Here's why it matters:

1. **Knowledge Sharing and Learning**: Developer communities are a great place to both share knowledge and learn from others. Engaging with fellow developers allows you to exchange ideas, tackle new challenges, and keep up with the latest trends in technology. It's a win-win situation where everyone benefits from mutual learning and problem-solving.

    o **Example**: By participating in discussions on StackOverflow or Reddit, you not only help others solve problems but also expose yourself to new approaches and best practices that can enhance your own skills.

2. **Building Relationships and Networking**: Engaging in developer communities enables you to build relationships with like-minded individuals. These relationships can lead to valuable career opportunities, collaborations, and partnerships. Networking in these spaces also allows you to connect with people who can offer advice, mentorship, and support.

   o **Example**: Contributing to a popular open-source project on GitHub or participating in discussions on Dev.to can introduce you to mentors or peers who may guide you in your career or collaborate on future projects.

3. **Increasing Your Visibility**: By actively participating and contributing to developer communities, you can significantly increase your visibility. Whether it's answering questions, writing blog posts, or sharing your experiences, the more you contribute, the more recognition you will gain within the community. This visibility can attract job opportunities, freelance gigs, or collaborations.

- Example: Being an active contributor on platforms like StackOverflow, where your answers receive high upvotes, establishes you as an authority and helps you get noticed by potential employers or collaborators.

4. **Demonstrating Expertise**: Participating in discussions, answering questions, and sharing insights helps you establish yourself as an expert in your area. When you solve problems for others or offer valuable insights, you prove your technical capabilities and problem-solving skills to the community, which enhances your personal brand.

- Example: If you're known for solving complex React issues on StackOverflow or explaining advanced Python concepts on Reddit, people will start to view you as a trusted expert in those technologies.

5. **Creating Long-Term Value**: The knowledge you contribute in communities like Dev.to or StackOverflow is accessible for years to come. Your contributions become a part of the collective knowledge base that can be referred to by others long after you've posted them. This long-term

value ensures that your personal brand continues to grow as more people find and benefit from your contributions.

- o **Example**: Your answer to a question about building a scalable Node.js application might get referenced by hundreds of developers over time, making you a recognized authority on that subject.

How to Contribute to StackOverflow, Reddit, Dev.to, and Other Online Communities

Contributing to online developer communities is an effective way to build your personal brand and network with other professionals. Here's how you can start contributing to major platforms:

1. StackOverflow

StackOverflow is one of the most well-known Q&A platforms for developers. It's a great place to showcase your expertise by answering questions, solving problems, and providing valuable solutions.

- **Answering   Questions**: Focus on answering questions related to your

173

expertise. Provide clear, well-explained, and actionable solutions that help others understand the problem and the solution. Use code snippets, examples, and explanations to make your answers thorough and valuable.

- o **Tip**: Start by answering questions that are tagged with your areas of expertise, such as "JavaScript," "React," "Python," or "Node.js." This makes it easier for you to offer solutions and engage with the community.

- **Ask Thoughtful Questions**: If you encounter challenges that others might also face, ask insightful questions. Engaging with the community through well-written questions can help others while also positioning you as someone who is actively involved in the community.

- o **Tip**: Be specific when asking questions. Include relevant code snippets, error messages, and your research efforts to ensure that your question is clear and likely to receive helpful responses.

- **Build Reputation**: The more you contribute, the more reputation points you earn on StackOverflow. This enhances your visibility and establishes your credibility within the community. High-reputation users often get their answers and posts featured more prominently, further increasing their reach.

2. Reddit (r/programming, r/learnprogramming, r/webdev, etc.)

Reddit is home to numerous developer-focused subreddits where developers of all skill levels can discuss trends, share resources, and seek advice. Here's how to get involved:

- **Participate in Discussions**: Join relevant subreddits, such as r/programming, r/learnprogramming, or r/webdev, and actively engage in discussions. Share your insights, contribute to technical conversations, and offer support to newcomers in the community.
  - o **Tip**: Stay respectful and constructive in your comments. Reddit communities thrive on collaboration, and making meaningful contributions is a great way to build relationships.

- **Share Resources and Tutorials**: Post valuable resources, tutorials, and guides to help others in the community. Whether it's a link to a blog post, an open-source project, or a video, providing helpful resources can establish you as a go-to person for information.
  - o **Example**: Posting a link to a tutorial you've written on building a full-stack app using React and Node.js can attract interest and lead to further engagement with other developers.
- **Host AMA (Ask Me Anything)**: As you build your reputation, consider hosting an AMA (Ask Me Anything) on relevant subreddits. Share your experience in a particular technology or project and invite the community to ask questions. This is a great way to increase your visibility and connect with others who share your interests.

3. Dev.to

Dev.to is a platform specifically designed for developers to share articles, tutorials, and engage in discussions. It's an excellent platform for building your brand as a technical writer or educator.

176

- **Write Articles and Tutorials**: Dev.to is a great place to write in-depth technical articles, share tutorials, or write about your developer journey. The platform has a large and engaged community that actively reads, comments, and shares articles related to software development.
  - o **Tip**: Focus on writing valuable content that solves real problems or explains complex concepts clearly. Engaging posts with examples, code snippets, and personal experiences tend to attract the most attention.
- **Engage in Discussions**: Read and comment on other developers' posts. Adding thoughtful comments to other articles can help you connect with like-minded individuals and demonstrate your expertise in specific topics.
  - o **Tip**: Regularly engage with posts that interest you, ask questions, and provide feedback or suggestions to enhance the conversation.
- **Join Dev.to Events and Challenges**: Dev.to frequently hosts coding challenges and community events, such as "100 Days of Code" or "Dev.to Writing Challenges." Participating in these

events can help you gain visibility and connect with other developers.

- o **Example**: Joining a challenge where you commit to learning a new framework or building a project for 30 days can help you develop new skills while expanding your network.

4. GitHub and Other Developer Platforms

GitHub is not just a place for hosting code—it's a social platform where developers collaborate, contribute to open-source projects, and share knowledge.

- **Contribute to Open Source**: Actively contributing to open-source projects on GitHub is one of the best ways to engage with the developer community. Whether you're fixing bugs, adding new features, or improving documentation, contributing to open-source projects is a great way to build your brand and gain recognition.
  - o **Tip**: Choose projects that align with your skills or areas you want to learn more about. Make sure your contributions are well-

documented and easy for others to understand.

- **Create and Share Projects**: Showcase your own projects on GitHub, whether they're personal projects, tools, or apps. Be sure to write clear README files, document your code well, and make your repositories accessible for collaboration.

  o **Example**: Share a personal project, like a portfolio website or a custom API, and invite others to contribute or offer feedback.

Examples of Developers Who Built Their Brands by Engaging with These Communities

1. **John Sonmez (Simple Programmer)** John Sonmez, the founder of Simple Programmer, built his personal brand by engaging with developers through his blog, YouTube channel, and StackOverflow contributions. His active participation in online communities and willingness to share his career advice helped him establish himself as a go-to resource for career development in tech.

- o **Key Takeaway**: John's willingness to answer questions, write blog posts, and create videos made him an influential voice in the software development community.

2. **Travis** **Fischer**

Travis Fischer is a well-known developer who built his brand through his contributions to open-source projects and his active presence on GitHub. By collaborating on widely-used libraries and tools, Travis earned recognition from peers and potential employers, which helped him grow his career.

- o **Key Takeaway**: Travis's focus on open-source and his consistent contributions to projects that matter to the community allowed him to establish a solid reputation as a reliable developer.

3. **Adam** **Wathan**

Adam Wathan is known for his work on the popular PHP framework Laravel and his blog posts on software development best practices. He gained recognition by writing about topics such as testing and code quality on platforms like Dev.to and Twitter, which led to a strong online following.

o **Key Takeaway**: Adam's success came from his dedication to providing valuable content and his active participation in online developer communities, positioning himself as an authority in PHP and web development.

Conclusion

Engaging with developer communities is a key component of building your personal brand and advancing your career as a developer. Whether you're answering questions on StackOverflow, participating in discussions on Reddit, writing tutorials on Dev.to, or contributing to open-source projects on GitHub, active involvement allows you to share your knowledge, network with others, and gain recognition within the tech community.

In the next chapter, we will explore how to build and sustain long-term relationships with mentors, collaborators, and industry leaders to further enhance your career and personal brand.

CHAPTER 16

BUILDING AN EMAIL LIST AND NEWSLETTER

How Building an Email List Can Help You Connect with Your Audience

Building an email list is one of the most effective ways to develop and maintain a connection with your audience. While social media platforms, blogs, and video content help you reach new audiences, email allows you to directly communicate with individuals who have already shown interest in your work. Here's why building an email list is a crucial strategy for your personal brand:

1. **Direct Communication with Your Audience**: Email is a direct channel to your audience, bypassing the algorithms that control what people see on social media platforms. When you send an email, you can be sure that it lands in your audience's inbox, allowing for more personalized and meaningful communication.

   o **Example**: A developer who creates weekly coding tips or resources can use email to send curated content directly to subscribers, ensuring they receive value regularly.

2. **Stronger Relationships and Trust**: Email is a more personal form of communication than social media or blog posts. By engaging with your audience through well-crafted emails, you can build trust over time. Providing value in your newsletters—whether through helpful content, tutorials, or exclusive insights—can help solidify your reputation as a trusted source of information.

   o **Example**: Sending out a personal message to thank your subscribers for their support or offering exclusive tips that can't be found on your blog fosters stronger relationships.

3. **High Engagement and Conversion Rates**: Email marketing has some of the highest engagement and conversion rates compared to other marketing channels. People who opt in to your email list are already interested in your content, making them more likely to engage with your newsletters and take the actions you want, such as clicking links, signing up for webinars, or purchasing your products.

   o **Example**: A developer who offers an online course can use email to announce special offers or promotions, leading to higher conversion rates compared to general social media marketing.

4. **Ownership of Your Audience**: On social media platforms, your reach and audience are subject to platform changes, such as algorithm updates. However, with an email list, you own your audience, and you can continue to reach them regardless of external factors. This provides greater control and long-term stability for your personal brand.

   o **Example**: If you've built a substantial email list, even if social media platforms change or become less effective, you still have a direct line to your audience through email.

5. **Nurturing Your Leads**: An email list allows you to nurture leads over time. Whether you're selling a product, offering a service, or promoting a course, email can be a way to continuously engage with your audience, share updates, and provide valuable content that moves them closer to becoming customers or collaborators.

   o **Example**: Developers offering paid technical courses can use their email list to nurture leads, provide sneak peeks of course content, and offer early-bird discounts to drive conversions.

Tips for Creating a Valuable Newsletter for Your Followers

Creating a valuable newsletter that resonates with your audience is key to ensuring that your email list remains engaged and continues to grow. Here are some tips to help you craft a newsletter that provides value:

1. Provide Consistent, High-Quality Content

The foundation of any successful newsletter is providing valuable, high-quality content. Your subscribers are likely to stay on your list if they find your content helpful, informative, or entertaining. You can share a range of content types, such as tutorials, tips, project updates, industry news, or personal experiences.

- **Tip**: Establish a consistent schedule for your newsletter (e.g., weekly, bi-weekly, or monthly) to keep your audience engaged and anticipate your next email.
- **Example**: A developer writing a newsletter about JavaScript might include tips for improving coding

skills, links to new tutorials, and insights on the latest JS frameworks.

2. Personalize Your Newsletter

Personalization helps your emails feel more human and tailored to your audience. Use your subscriber's name in the email and segment your list if necessary to ensure that you send relevant content to different audience groups. For instance, if you have a newsletter about both front-end and back-end development, you can segment your email list so that subscribers only receive the content that aligns with their interests.

- **Tip**: Personalization goes beyond just using your subscriber's name. If you have more data (like what topics they engage with), use it to send targeted content that resonates with them.
- **Example**: A developer newsletter focused on web development could send different content based on the subscriber's previous interactions. For example, one group might receive more front-end tutorials, while another group might get back-end tips.

186

3. Include Calls-to-Action (CTAs)

Every newsletter should include a clear call-to-action (CTA) that guides your subscribers toward the next step. Whether it's encouraging them to check out a new blog post, register for a webinar, or purchase your latest course, a strong CTA directs your audience toward further engagement.

- **Tip**: Make sure your CTA is clear and actionable. Instead of vague CTAs like "Check out my latest work," try something like "Click here to learn how to build a scalable React app."
- **Example**: A developer who has written a new article could include a CTA like, "Read my latest tutorial on building a full-stack app with Node.js," encouraging subscribers to engage with the content.

4. Share Exclusive Content or Offers

Give your subscribers something extra that they can't get anywhere else. This could be early access to content, exclusive discounts, free downloads, or special behind-the-scenes insights. This not only adds value but also makes subscribers feel special and appreciated.

- **Tip**: Regularly offer something exclusive to your email list, like a free eBook, a discount code for your course, or a sneak peek at a new project.

- **Example**: If you're offering a paid course, give your email subscribers an exclusive early-bird discount or access to a free webinar that introduces the course topics.

5. Keep the Design Clean and Easy to Read

Your email's design should be clean, professional, and easy to read. Avoid overwhelming your subscribers with too much text or complex designs. Use clear headings, bullet points, and concise paragraphs to make the content scannable. Mobile optimization is crucial since many people read emails on their phones.

- **Tip**: Use simple, visually appealing templates or email marketing platforms like Mailchimp or ConvertKit, which offer easy-to-use tools to design your newsletters.

- **Example**: A technical newsletter could include concise code snippets, clear headings, and short descriptions of each tutorial or article to make the content easy to digest on both mobile and desktop devices.

Real Examples of Developers Who Successfully Use Newsletters for Branding

1. **Adam Wathan (Tailwind CSS)**
   Adam Wathan, creator of the popular Tailwind CSS framework, uses his newsletter to engage with the web development community. His newsletter includes updates on Tailwind, personal insights, and links to his educational content. By sharing valuable content and personal stories, Adam has built a strong following through his newsletter.
   - **Key Takeaway**: Adam's success with his newsletter comes from providing useful, relevant content to his subscribers while also offering insights into his journey with Tailwind CSS. This adds authenticity and builds trust with his audience.

2. **Chris Coyier (CSS-Tricks)**
   Chris Coyier, the founder of CSS-Tricks, has used his newsletter to provide updates on web development techniques, resources, and blog content. His newsletter acts as a curated list of

helpful articles, tutorials, and news from the world of web development. Chris's ability to share valuable, relevant content has helped him build a large and engaged audience.

- o **Key Takeaway**: Chris has successfully used his newsletter to provide consistent value, positioning himself as a trusted resource for developers. By sharing hand-picked content, he keeps his audience engaged and looking forward to his updates.

3. **Wes Bos (JavaScript30, WesBos.com)** Wes Bos, a well-known JavaScript educator, has used his email list to grow his personal brand and promote his courses. He regularly sends valuable coding tips, free tutorials, and updates on his latest projects. His email list has been instrumental in promoting his paid courses, such as JavaScript30, which offers free 30-day coding challenges.

- o **Key Takeaway**: Wes uses his email list not just for promotion but also for adding value to his subscribers through free challenges and content. This approach has helped him build a loyal following that eagerly anticipates his updates.

4. **Mosh   Hamedani   (CodeWithMosh)**

Mosh Hamedani, a software engineer and educator, has built his personal brand largely through email marketing. His newsletters share updates on his online courses, new videos, and exclusive offers. Mosh also uses his email list to promote his coding courses and connect with his audience through personal messages and insights.

- o **Key Takeaway**: Mosh's email list is a core part of his strategy to promote his courses and build a deeper connection with his students. By offering exclusive content and personalized communication, he keeps his subscribers engaged and loyal.

Conclusion

Building an email list and creating a valuable newsletter is an essential part of growing your personal brand as a developer. By providing consistent, high-quality content that adds value to your subscribers, you can foster strong relationships, increase engagement, and establish yourself as a trusted expert in your field. Whether you're sharing coding tutorials, career advice, or personal stories, a well-crafted email list can be one of the most powerful tools for building a long-term connection with your audience.

In the next chapter, we will explore how to monetize your personal brand as a developer and turn your expertise into sustainable income streams.

CHAPTER 17

OFFERING PAID CONTENT (COURSES, WORKSHOPS)

How to Create and Monetize Online Courses or Workshops

Creating and monetizing online courses or workshops is one of the most effective ways for developers to leverage their expertise and generate income. Online education offers the potential to reach a global audience, and with the rise of e-learning platforms, it's easier than ever to package your knowledge into a course or workshop format. Here's how you can create and monetize your own courses or workshops:

1. Choose a Niche Topic

- **Focus on Your Expertise**: Select a topic that you are deeply knowledgeable about and that is in demand in the market. The more specialized your topic, the easier it will be to target a specific audience.
- **Consider Audience Pain Points**: Think about the common problems or questions your audience faces. Addressing these challenges with a clear solution is

key to creating valuable content that people are willing to pay for.

- **Example**: If you're an expert in JavaScript, a course on "Mastering JavaScript for Beginners" or a workshop focused on "Advanced JavaScript Concepts" might attract a niche group of learners.

2. Plan Your Course or Workshop Structure

- **Break It Down into Modules**: Organize your content into logical, bite-sized modules or lessons that build upon one another. A well-structured course improves the learning experience and keeps students engaged.
- **Add Practical Exercises**: Courses that offer real-world, hands-on exercises tend to have higher engagement. Consider including quizzes, coding challenges, and projects that help students apply what they've learned.
- **Include Multimedia**: Mix up your content with video lessons, slides, written materials, and even audio to accommodate different learning styles.
- **Example**: A course on web development might have modules on HTML, CSS, JavaScript, and building a simple web app. Each module could include video

tutorials, downloadable code snippets, and a final project for students to submit.

3. Create High-Quality Content

- **Invest in Good Equipment**: High-quality video and audio are essential for creating a professional course. Invest in a good microphone, screen recording software, and video editing tools to ensure your content is clear and engaging.
- **Engage with Visuals**: Visuals like slides, code snippets, and demonstrations are key to enhancing your course. Use clear, easy-to-follow diagrams or flowcharts to explain complex concepts.
- **Example**: If you're teaching React, create step-by-step videos where you code live, explaining your thought process, with side-by-side code examples for students to follow.

4. Price Your Course or Workshop

- **Consider the Value**: Price your course based on the value you're offering. If your course is highly specialized or provides deep, in-depth knowledge, you can price it higher than a beginner-level course.

- **Competitive Pricing**: Research similar courses in your niche to understand the market rate and ensure that your pricing is competitive.

- **Offer Discounts or Early-Bird Pricing**: Offering promotional discounts or early-bird pricing can create urgency and attract initial sign-ups.

- **Example**: A basic course might be priced at $30, while an advanced workshop with live feedback could be priced at $150.

5. Market Your Course

- **Leverage Your Existing Audience**: If you already have a blog, YouTube channel, or email list, use those platforms to promote your course. Create landing pages with compelling calls-to-action (CTAs) and share testimonials from early users to build credibility.

- **Use Social Media**: Promote your course on social media platforms like Twitter, LinkedIn, Instagram, and Facebook. Share sneak peeks of your course content, success stories from students, and limited-time offers to encourage sign-ups.

- **Create a Free Preview**: Offering a free mini-course, webinar, or preview of your content is a great way to attract potential customers. A free sample helps build trust and gives people a taste of what they can expect from the full course.

- **Example**: You could create a free webinar or blog post that covers a topic from your course and invite viewers to sign up for the full course for a special discount.

Platforms to Host and Sell Your Courses

Several platforms allow developers to host, sell, and distribute online courses and workshops. These platforms provide built-in tools for content delivery, marketing, and payment processing, making it easier to focus on creating high-quality content. Here are some of the most popular platforms:

1. Udemy

- **Overview**: Udemy is one of the largest online learning platforms, with millions of students and a broad marketplace for instructors. It provides a massive reach and allows instructors to set their own pricing and access to promotional tools.
- **Pros**:

- o Large user base.
- o Built-in marketing tools to help promote your course.
- o Ability to price courses as you see fit.
- **Cons**:
  - o Udemy takes a commission on sales, which can be significant (50% for Udemy-sold courses).
  - o Less control over branding and user data.
- **Tip**: To maximize your earnings on Udemy, promote your course outside of the platform and use Udemy's own marketing tools to increase visibility.

2. Teachable

- **Overview**: Teachable is a popular platform that allows creators to build and sell their own online courses. It offers customizable sales pages, integration with payment systems, and marketing tools.
- **Pros**:
  - o Complete control over pricing and sales.
  - o Ability to brand your course with your own domain and design.
  - o Full ownership of student data.

- **Cons**:
  - Requires more effort to attract students, as it lacks a built-in marketplace like Udemy.
- **Tip**: Teachable is ideal for developers who already have an audience or a personal brand and want more control over their course content and sales.

3. Skillshare

- **Overview**: Skillshare is a community-driven platform that focuses on creative and technical skills. Courses on Skillshare are generally shorter and often involve hands-on projects.
- **Pros**:
  - A large, engaged community of learners.
  - Payment based on views and student engagement.
- **Cons**:
  - Less control over pricing and revenue.
  - Typically requires producing shorter, project-based courses.
- **Tip**: Skillshare is a great platform for developers who want to create short, engaging lessons and attract a global audience.

4. Gumroad

- **Overview**: Gumroad is a platform for selling digital products, including courses, eBooks, and other digital content. It's very flexible, allowing you to set your own prices and use the platform for direct sales.
- **Pros**:
    - Complete control over pricing and sales.
    - Low fees (Gumroad takes 3.5% + 30¢ per transaction).
    - Great for selling one-off products like workshops or eBooks.
- **Cons**:
    - Doesn't have the marketing tools or user base of platforms like Udemy.
    - More effort is needed to drive traffic to your Gumroad page.
- **Tip**: Use Gumroad for more personalized or niche courses, and combine it with your existing audience to maximize sales.

5. Podia

- **Overview**: Podia is a platform designed for creators who want to sell courses, memberships, and digital products. It's known for its simplicity and ease of use.

- **Pros**:
  - Complete control over your content and pricing.
  - No transaction fees on sales.
  - Membership options for recurring income.
- **Cons**:
  - Requires some initial effort to grow an audience.
  - Lacks the built-in audience that platforms like Udemy offer.
- **Tip**: Podia works well for developers who want to build a membership-based course or offer a subscription model alongside one-off courses.

Case Studies of Developers Who Transitioned from Free Content to Paid Offerings

1. **Brad Traversy (Traversy Media)** Brad Traversy, a well-known web development educator, began by sharing free tutorials on his YouTube channel, Traversy Media. Over time, he created paid courses that offered more in-depth content. His courses on Udemy have become highly successful, and he has

also transitioned to selling his own courses on platforms like Teachable.

- o **Key Takeaway**: Brad's success came from building an audience through consistent, high-quality free content before transitioning to paid offerings. His personal brand and loyal following made it easier to monetize his courses.

2. **Mosh Hamedani (CodeWithMosh)** Mosh Hamedani started by offering free content on his YouTube channel and through blog posts. After building a solid following, he launched paid courses on platforms like Udemy and his own site. Mosh's courses on full-stack development, React, and JavaScript have been extremely successful.

- o **Key Takeaway**: Mosh successfully used his free content as a lead magnet to build trust and credibility before offering paid courses. He also strategically used his email list to market his paid courses directly to his audience.

3. **Kent C. Dodds (Kent C. Dodds)** Kent C. Dodds, a prominent React and JavaScript educator, began offering free tutorials and content through his blog

and YouTube. Later, he transitioned into paid content through his own platform, with courses such as "Epic React" becoming a significant part of his revenue.

- **Key Takeaway**: Kent's journey from free content to paid offerings shows the importance of building a solid foundation with free resources. His paid courses are highly regarded due to his strong personal brand and trust built through his free content.

Conclusion

Creating and monetizing online courses or workshops is a great way to turn your expertise into a sustainable income stream while building your personal brand. By selecting a niche, creating high-quality content, and leveraging platforms like Udemy, Teachable, and Gumroad, you can start offering value to your audience and growing your career. With the right strategies, you can successfully transition from providing free content to building profitable paid offerings.

In the next chapter, we will explore strategies for scaling your personal brand and expanding your business opportunities as a developer.

CHAPTER 18

PERSONAL BRANDING THROUGH FREELANCE WORK

How Freelancing Can Build Your Brand and Expand Your Career Opportunities

Freelancing is an excellent way to build and expand your personal brand as a developer. By working with a variety of clients, taking on diverse projects, and showcasing your skills in different contexts, you can significantly boost your visibility and reputation. Here's how freelancing can help build your personal brand and create more career opportunities:

1. **Building a Diverse Portfolio**: Freelancing allows you to work on a wide range of projects across different industries. This gives you the chance to develop a diverse portfolio that demonstrates your versatility. Whether you're building websites, developing apps, or working with emerging technologies, your portfolio will reflect the breadth of your skills.

○ **Example**: If you're a web developer, taking on projects that involve front-end, back-end, and full-stack development allows you to showcase a broader skillset, attracting more potential clients who need different services.

2. **Gaining   Recognition**: By delivering high-quality work on freelance platforms, you can quickly gain recognition within the freelance community. Positive reviews, client testimonials, and repeat business all contribute to your reputation. This recognition can help you stand out in a crowded marketplace and attract higher-paying clients.

○ **Example**: A developer with consistently great reviews on a platform like Upwork is likely to be viewed as more reliable and trustworthy by prospective clients, leading to more job offers.

3. **Building   Relationships   and   Networking**: Freelancing allows you to build relationships with clients, other developers, and potential collaborators. These relationships can be incredibly valuable for future opportunities. Satisfied clients might refer you to others or even offer you ongoing work. Freelance

platforms often encourage community interaction, where developers can exchange tips and ideas.

- o **Example**: A freelance developer who consistently delivers excellent work and communicates well with clients is likely to form long-term relationships with clients who return for future projects.

4. **Developing a Personal Brand**: Freelancers have the unique opportunity to shape their own personal brand. By consistently delivering quality work, showcasing your expertise on platforms like LinkedIn, and engaging in discussions within developer communities, you can position yourself as an expert in your field. This helps attract clients who value your specific skills and knowledge.

- o **Example**: A developer specializing in React may brand themselves as a "React expert" on their freelance profile, attracting clients specifically looking for that expertise.

5. **Increasing Career Opportunities**: Freelancing often leads to other career opportunities, including full-time offers, consulting gigs, or partnerships with other freelancers. As you build your reputation, you may be approached by

companies or entrepreneurs who want to bring you onto their teams or collaborate with you on larger projects.

- o **Example**: A freelance developer who excels at building scalable applications for startups may be invited to work with a growing tech company on a permanent basis.

Setting Your Freelance Profile on Platforms Like Upwork or Fiverr

Freelancing platforms like Upwork and Fiverr are key to building your personal brand and attracting clients. These platforms provide a space where you can showcase your skills, apply for jobs, and engage with clients. Here's how you can set up an effective freelance profile on these platforms:

1. Creating a Standout Profile

Your profile is the first impression potential clients will have of you, so it's important to make it as professional and attractive as possible. Here's how to craft a profile that stands out:

- **Choose the Right Niche**: Focus on your specific area of expertise, whether it's web development, mobile app development, or cybersecurity. This helps clients quickly identify your strengths and understand how you can meet their needs.

  o **Tip**: If you specialize in a specific technology, like React or Django, make sure to highlight that in your profile title and description.

- **Write a Compelling Bio**: Your bio should clearly explain who you are, your experience, and what makes you unique. Focus on how your skills can solve problems for potential clients. Include your key achievements and emphasize your ability to deliver quality results.

  o **Tip**: Keep it client-focused. Instead of listing all of your technical skills, explain how your skills will help the client solve specific problems.

  o **Example**: "I'm a full-stack developer with over 5 years of experience building custom web applications. I specialize in React and Node.js, and I focus on creating scalable, performance-optimized solutions that help businesses grow."

- **Highlight Your Skills and Expertise**: Be sure to list all the relevant skills you have, including technical tools, programming languages, and frameworks. Take time to ensure your profile showcases the tools you're proficient in so that clients can see your full capabilities.

  o **Tip**: Include any certifications, training, or notable projects that back up your skills.

- **Showcase Your Portfolio**: One of the most important aspects of your freelance profile is your portfolio. Upload examples of your past work, whether they're websites, apps, or other projects. If you don't have client work to show, create personal projects or contribute to open-source projects.

  o **Tip**: Ensure that your portfolio is updated and reflects the type of work you want to attract. For example, if you want more freelance React jobs, make sure your portfolio highlights your best React projects.

2. Setting Competitive Pricing

Freelance platforms offer the flexibility to set your own rates, but it's important to set competitive pricing that reflects your skills, experience, and market demand. Here's how to set your pricing:

- **Research the Market**: Look at other freelancers with similar skills and experience to get a sense of the going rates. On platforms like Upwork and Fiverr, you can see the rates of top-rated freelancers, which can help you determine where to position yourself.
  - o **Tip**: Don't underprice your services just to land clients. Competitive rates that reflect your expertise will attract clients who are willing to pay for quality work.
- **Start with a Competitive Rate**: If you're just starting on a platform and don't have much of a track record, it's okay to set a lower introductory rate to attract clients. As you build reviews and gain experience, you can gradually increase your rates.
  - o **Example**: A new freelancer might start by offering their services at $30/hour, but after

211

accumulating positive reviews and establishing a reputation, they can increase their rate to $50 or more per hour.

3. Writing Proposals and Bidding on Jobs

On platforms like Upwork, clients often post job listings, and freelancers need to submit proposals to be considered. Here's how you can write winning proposals:

- **Personalize Your Proposal**: Tailor each proposal to the specific job. Avoid generic responses. Address the client's needs directly and explain how you can provide the best solution for their project.
  - **Tip**: Show that you understand the client's requirements. Mention specific technologies or methodologies you'll use to address their problems.
- **Highlight Relevant Experience**: Share examples from your portfolio or previous work that are relevant to the job at hand. This shows the client that you have the right experience and can deliver results.

212

- **Set Clear Expectations**: In your proposal, outline the scope of the work, timelines, and expected deliverables. Being transparent helps build trust and reduces the chances of misunderstandings down the line.

- **Be Professional**: Keep your tone professional and respectful. A well-written proposal that demonstrates your professionalism increases your chances of being hired.

Real-World Examples of Developers Who Grew Their Brand Through Freelancing

1. **Chris from CodingPhase**
   Chris from CodingPhase started his freelancing career by offering web development services on platforms like Upwork. By delivering high-quality projects and showcasing his expertise in web development, he quickly grew his reputation and built a large following. Today, Chris runs his own successful YouTube channel and offers online courses, leveraging his freelancing experience to build his personal brand.

o **Key Takeaway**: Chris grew his personal brand through consistent freelancing, building a reputation for reliability, quality work, and expertise in web development.

2. **Hassan, a Python Freelancer**
   Hassan transitioned from freelance work on Fiverr to building a personal brand as a Python expert. He started by offering simple Python scripting services but, over time, took on larger, more complex projects. Through his excellent work and consistent client feedback, he attracted attention from high-paying clients and turned freelancing into a full-time career.

   o **Key Takeaway**: Hassan's ability to diversify his projects and deliver consistent, quality results helped him establish himself as an expert in Python, growing his brand through freelancing platforms.

3. **Anne from Upwork (UX/UI Designer)**
   Anne started her freelancing journey on Upwork as a beginner UX/UI designer. By continually upgrading her skills and offering high-quality design services, she quickly received positive reviews from clients. As she gained more experience and built a portfolio,

Anne started landing larger projects with top-tier companies, helping her transition from freelancing to establishing her own design consultancy.

- o **Key Takeaway**: Anne's focus on quality work, client communication, and ongoing skill development helped her move from a beginner freelancer to an in-demand consultant.

Conclusion

Freelancing offers developers the chance to build a personal brand, expand career opportunities, and increase visibility in the tech community. By setting up an attractive profile on freelancing platforms like Upwork or Fiverr, offering valuable services, and delivering exceptional work, you can leverage freelancing to grow your brand and career. Consistent quality work, networking, and building a solid reputation on these platforms will help you attract new opportunities and clients, ultimately establishing you as a recognized expert in your field.

In the next chapter, we will explore strategies for scaling your personal brand and turning your freelance work into long-term business growth.

CHAPTER 19

COLLABORATING WITH OTHER DEVELOPERS

Why Collaboration is Key to Growing Your Brand and Learning

Collaboration is one of the most powerful strategies for developers to grow their personal brand, expand their skill set, and build strong professional networks. In today's fast-evolving tech landscape, working with other developers opens the door to numerous opportunities. Here's why collaboration is essential for both personal and professional growth:

1. **Expanding Knowledge and Skills**: Collaboration allows you to learn from others with different skill sets and experiences. When you work with developers who specialize in areas that are outside your expertise, you get to enhance your own skill set and broaden your knowledge. For example, if you're a front-end developer, collaborating with a back-end developer will expose you to new programming languages, tools, and approaches.

217

- **Example**: A full-stack developer collaborating with a machine learning expert might gain insight into using data science techniques in web development, which can be a valuable skill set in today's tech job market.

2. **Exposure to New Ideas and Perspectives**: Working with other developers from diverse backgrounds can lead to fresh ideas and innovative solutions to problems. Different perspectives can help you approach challenges from unique angles and think outside the box. Collaboration often sparks creativity and leads to more efficient or novel ways of solving problems.

   - **Example**: A team of developers collaborating on a new app might come up with unique features or an improved user interface through group brainstorming, incorporating ideas that none of them would have considered alone.

3. **Building a Strong Professional Network**: Collaboration helps you build relationships with other developers, creating valuable connections within the industry. These relationships can lead to

future collaborations, job offers, referrals, and even business partnerships. The more people you work with, the more opportunities you will have for career advancement.

- o **Example**: A developer who collaborates on open-source projects or joins hackathons can meet peers and mentors who help them get hired by a top tech company or introduce them to influential people in the industry.

4. **Establishing Yourself as a Team Player**: By collaborating effectively, you demonstrate to potential clients or employers that you are a team player who can work well in group settings. This is an important skill, as most development projects require teamwork and coordination. Building this reputation helps enhance your professional image and brand.

- o **Example**: A developer who has experience working in agile development teams and delivering projects in collaboration with others will be seen as someone who can thrive in a collaborative environment, making them more attractive to potential clients or employers.

5. **Improving Communication and Collaboration Skills**:

Working with other developers helps improve your communication and collaboration skills. It forces you to explain your ideas clearly, listen to others, and resolve conflicts constructively. Effective communication is essential when working in teams, and collaboration helps refine this skill.

- o **Example**: During a pair programming session, developers practice communicating their thought processes clearly, which helps them explain technical concepts in simple terms—a skill that is invaluable when interacting with clients or non-technical stakeholders.

How to Find and Collaborate with Other Developers on Projects

Finding other developers to collaborate with may seem daunting, but there are numerous platforms and strategies that can help you connect with like-minded individuals for project collaboration. Here's how you can find and collaborate with other developers:

1. Join Open-Source Projects

Open-source projects are an excellent way to collaborate with developers globally. These projects often have a collaborative nature, with multiple developers working together to contribute code, solve issues, and improve software. Contributing to open-source projects gives you the opportunity to work on real-world projects and gain visibility in the tech community.

- **Where to Find Projects**: Platforms like GitHub, GitLab, and Bitbucket host a wide range of open-source projects. You can start by browsing repositories that align with your interests or expertise and contribute to them by fixing bugs, adding features, or improving documentation.
  - o **Tip**: Look for projects labeled "good first issue" to find beginner-friendly tasks that help you get started without feeling overwhelmed.
- **Example**: A developer interested in React might contribute to a popular React-based project on GitHub, collaborating with other developers to fix bugs and add features.

2. Attend Meetups and Conferences

Attending developer meetups, conferences, and hackathons is a great way to meet other developers who are looking to collaborate on projects. These events often feature networking sessions, workshops, and collaborative activities that encourage participants to team up and work on real-world problems.

- **Tip**: Look for events or groups in your area that focus on your specific interests, whether it's mobile development, web development, or machine learning. Websites like Meetup.com or Eventbrite often list tech-related meetups and conferences.
- **Example**: At a local hackathon, developers often form teams to build a project in a short period. This fosters collaboration and allows you to work with people who have diverse skill sets.

3. Participate in Online Developer Communities

Online communities and forums are a great way to meet other developers and find collaboration opportunities. Platforms like Stack Overflow, Reddit (e.g., r/programming, r/learnprogramming), and Dev.to allow you to engage with developers worldwide, share your knowledge, and connect with others who may want to collaborate on projects.

- **Tip**: Engage in discussions, offer solutions to problems, and share your expertise in these communities. This helps you gain credibility and build relationships with fellow developers who may reach out to you for future collaborations.
- **Example**: A developer who frequently contributes to discussions about Python programming on Reddit might be invited to collaborate on a Python-based project or join a team working on a new open-source tool.

4. Collaborate on Freelance Platforms

Freelance platforms like Upwork, Fiverr, and Toptal provide an opportunity to work with other developers on paid projects. These platforms allow you to team up with other freelancers or even work with clients who are looking for development teams.

- **Tip**: Look for collaboration opportunities in job listings or post your own offering to find other developers with complementary skills. For example, if you specialize in front-end development, look for opportunities to collaborate with back-end developers.

- **Example**: A freelance developer specializing in UX/UI design might collaborate with a back-end developer to create a full-stack web application for a client, allowing them to leverage each other's expertise.

5. Build Your Own Collaborative Projects

If you can't find a collaboration that suits your interests, create your own! Start a project and invite other developers to join. Whether it's a new tool, app, or open-source initiative, creating your own project and inviting collaborators can lead to valuable partnerships and opportunities.

- **Tip**: Use platforms like GitHub to host and manage the project, and create clear documentation and guidelines for other contributors. Make the project open to contributions and promote it on social media or developer forums.
- **Example**: You could start a project to develop a new, open-source library for data visualization and invite

other developers who are interested in data science or web development to contribute.

Examples of Successful Collaborations and Partnerships in the Tech Industry

1. **The React Ecosystem (Jordan Walke and Other Contributors)**

    React, developed by Jordan Walke at Facebook, is one of the most successful open-source collaborations in the tech industry. It was created as an internal project but grew through contributions from the developer community. React's success is largely due to its active community of contributors, who continuously enhance and expand its capabilities.

    o **Key Takeaway**: React's rise to prominence showcases how open-source collaboration can lead to the creation of highly successful, widely-used tools. Developers who contributed to React gained recognition, furthering their careers and personal brands.

2. **The Django Framework (Adrian Holovaty and Simon   Willison)**

    Django, a popular web framework for Python, was

developed by Adrian Holovaty and Simon Willison. Over time, the framework grew through contributions from developers around the world. The collaborative nature of the Django project helped it become one of the most used frameworks in web development today.

- o **Key Takeaway**: The success of Django illustrates the power of collaboration in building robust, widely-adopted technologies. Developers who contributed to Django have built strong personal brands and expanded their professional networks as a result.

3. **GitHub and the Open-Source Community** GitHub itself is a prime example of a platform built on collaboration. By offering a space for developers to share, collaborate, and contribute to open-source projects, GitHub has become a hub for developers to network and showcase their skills. Many developers have built their personal brands by contributing to popular projects hosted on GitHub.

- o **Key Takeaway**: GitHub's collaborative environment has led to the success of countless open-source projects and has allowed developers to build their personal brands by contributing to well-known projects.

Conclusion

Collaboration is an essential element of building your personal brand as a developer. By working with other developers on open-source projects, attending meetups, engaging in online communities, and collaborating on freelance platforms, you can enhance your skills, grow your network, and increase your visibility in the tech industry. Successful collaborations can lead to long-term professional relationships, business opportunities, and the recognition you need to advance your career.

In the next chapter, we will explore strategies for maintaining and expanding your personal brand as a developer in the long term.

CHAPTER 20

BECOMING A CONSULTANT

How to Transition from a Developer to a Consultant

Making the transition from being a developer to a consultant is a natural next step for many professionals looking to scale their careers and increase their impact in the tech industry. While being a developer involves executing code and working on projects, consulting focuses on advising clients, solving complex problems, and providing strategic insights. Here's how you can successfully make the transition to consulting:

1. Build Deep Expertise in Your Niche

- **Specialization is Key**: The most successful consultants are those who have developed deep expertise in a specific niche. Whether it's mobile app development, DevOps, or machine learning, specializing in a specific area gives you the credibility and authority needed to charge higher fees and attract clients looking for specific expertise.

- **Example**: If you're a web developer who has extensive experience with React, you could position yourself as a React expert, advising companies on how to scale their React-based applications or improve performance.

- **Tip**: Take time to master your niche through continuous learning, attending conferences, and contributing to industry discussions. Keep your knowledge current by staying up-to-date with trends, new technologies, and best practices.

2. Establish a Personal Brand

- **Leverage Your Online Presence**: Before you can position yourself as a consultant, you need to establish a personal brand. Use platforms like LinkedIn, GitHub, and Twitter to showcase your expertise, share valuable content, and engage with the developer community. This helps create visibility and authority in your field, which is essential when attracting consulting opportunities.

- **Tip**: Regularly publish blog posts, videos, or tutorials about your niche. By sharing knowledge, you demonstrate your expertise and establish yourself as a thought leader.

- **Example**: A developer with a blog focused on optimizing Node.js performance could attract businesses that are facing scaling challenges with their web applications and are seeking expert advice.

3. Network and Build Relationships

- **Leverage Existing Relationships**: As you build your personal brand, networking becomes crucial. Start by reaching out to your professional network—former colleagues, clients, and industry connections. Let them know that you're offering consulting services. Word-of-mouth referrals can be a powerful way to land your first consulting gigs.

- **Tip**: Attend industry events, participate in online communities, and offer advice or help to others. Building strong relationships with peers, clients, and industry influencers will increase your chances of getting consulting opportunities.

- **Example**: If you've worked on projects with various companies, reconnecting with those businesses and offering strategic advice on their tech stacks or architecture can lead to consulting work.

4. Create a Consulting Package and Pricing Structure

- **Define Your Offerings**: Clearly define what services you will provide as a consultant. This could include code audits, process improvement, technology advice, or training sessions for teams. Having a well-defined service offering helps potential clients understand what they can expect from you.

- **Tip**: Create different pricing packages based on the scope of the project. You might offer an hourly rate for short-term consultations or fixed-price packages for long-term projects.

- **Example**: A consultant with expertise in cloud migration could offer a fixed-price package for businesses wanting to move to the cloud, with a set fee for the assessment, implementation plan, and execution phase.

5. Start Small with Short-Term Gigs

- **Take on Small Consulting Projects**: In the beginning, it's important to take on smaller, lower-risk consulting projects. These projects can help you build your portfolio, gain client testimonials, and improve your consulting skills. As you gain experience, you can gradually scale to larger, higher-paying clients.

- **Tip**: Offer to work with startups or small businesses that may have limited budgets but need expert advice. These types of clients can give you the opportunity to prove your value and expand your consulting practice.

- **Example**: If you're a front-end developer, start with small consulting projects helping small businesses optimize their websites for performance or accessibility, and then gradually move to more complex web development challenges.

Positioning Yourself as an Expert in Your Niche to Attract Consulting Gigs

Successfully positioning yourself as an expert in your niche is key to attracting consulting gigs. Here are steps you can take to make yourself more visible and credible in your field:

1. Write a Book or eBook

- **Share Your Knowledge**: Writing a book or eBook about your area of expertise is a powerful way to position yourself as a subject-matter expert. A book helps establish credibility, and it serves as a marketing tool for attracting clients who are looking for experts with proven knowledge.

- **Tip**: If you're not ready to write an entire book, consider writing an in-depth guide or tutorial as an eBook that you can offer for free in exchange for email subscriptions or as a lead magnet.

- **Example**: A developer who writes a book on "Building Scalable Applications with React" could position themselves as an authority in the React community, attracting clients who want advice on scaling their React-based projects.

2. Publish Case Studies and Success Stories

- **Show Off Your Results**: Publishing case studies that showcase the results you've achieved for clients is an excellent way to build your reputation. Case studies demonstrate your ability to solve problems and deliver results, which is critical for attracting new clients.

- **Tip**: For each consulting project, document the challenges, the solutions you provided, and the impact of your work. Use this information to create detailed case studies that highlight your problem-solving and technical expertise.

- **Example**: If you helped a company streamline their development process by introducing continuous integration, a case study showing how you reduced deployment time and improved quality can help potential clients see the value you bring.

3. Offer Free Webinars and Workshops

- **Provide Value Through Education**: Hosting free webinars or workshops on a subject within your niche is a great way to demonstrate your expertise and build a following. These events also provide an opportunity to interact directly with potential clients and showcase your problem-solving abilities.

- **Tip**: Promote your webinars or workshops through your email list, social media, and LinkedIn. Use the event to build relationships with attendees and offer them consulting services afterward.

- **Example**: A developer with expertise in security best practices might offer a free workshop on "How to Secure Your Web Application," attracting clients who need help implementing security measures.

4. Build Your Own Website

- **Create an Online Presence**: Your website serves as a professional portfolio, showcasing your consulting services, client testimonials, case studies, and content that demonstrates your expertise. A well-designed website is essential for positioning yourself as an authority in your niche.

- **Tip**: Make sure your website is optimized for SEO, using keywords related to your expertise. Include a blog section where you can share your insights, tips, and case studies.

- **Example**: A web developer specializing in e-commerce could have a website showcasing their work, with a blog that discusses trends in e-commerce development and practical tips for optimizing online stores.

Real Stories of Developers Who Made a Successful Shift to Consulting

1. **David Heinemeier Hansson (Basecamp)** David Heinemeier Hansson, the creator of Ruby on Rails, transitioned from being a developer to a well-respected consultant in the software industry. His deep expertise in Ruby on Rails and his success with the Basecamp platform led to consulting opportunities with companies seeking guidance on building scalable applications.

   o **Key Takeaway**: David successfully built his consulting career by leveraging his deep technical expertise and building a solid reputation through his open-source contributions and successful products.

2. **Sarah Drasner (Vue.js, Web Animation Expert)** Sarah Drasner, a renowned expert in Vue.js and web animations, transitioned to consulting after building a solid personal brand. By contributing to the Vue.js framework, writing articles, and speaking at conferences, Sarah established herself as an authority in front-end development. This reputation led to

high-profile consulting gigs, where she helps companies implement advanced web animations and Vue.js integrations.

- o **Key Takeaway**: Sarah's transition to consulting was fueled by her active presence in the developer community, her contributions to open-source projects, and her ability to position herself as an expert in a specialized area.

3. **Kent C. Dodds (Testing JavaScript, React Expert)** Kent C. Dodds, a JavaScript educator, made the transition from being a full-time developer to a successful consultant by creating a course on testing JavaScript. His ability to teach complex topics in a simple, engaging way helped him attract consulting opportunities from companies seeking to improve their testing practices and React applications.

- o **Key Takeaway**: Kent's successful shift to consulting was facilitated by his reputation as an educator and his focus on a niche (JavaScript testing). His courses, workshops, and personal brand helped him establish authority in his field.

Conclusion

Transitioning from a developer to a consultant can significantly enhance your career, allowing you to leverage your expertise, increase your income, and create lasting relationships with clients. By positioning yourself as an expert in your niche, building a strong personal brand, and using strategic marketing techniques, you can attract consulting gigs that not only pay well but also provide personal fulfillment and career growth. The success stories of developers who have made the shift to consulting show that with the right approach, expertise, and dedication, you can build a rewarding career as a consultant in the tech industry.

In the next chapter, we will explore how to maintain long-term success in your consulting career and ensure sustainable growth and profitability.

CHAPTER 21

LEVERAGING PAID ADVERTISING FOR BRAND GROWTH

How to Use Ads (Google, LinkedIn, etc.) to Increase Visibility

Paid advertising is one of the most effective ways to increase the visibility of your personal brand and attract new opportunities as a developer. Whether you're looking to promote your consulting services, attract new clients, or build a larger following for your content, ads on platforms like Google, LinkedIn, and other social media networks can help you reach a highly targeted audience. Here's how you can use paid advertising to grow your brand:

1. Understand the Platform's Reach and Audience

Different platforms cater to different audiences. Knowing which platform is most suitable for your goals is essential in creating an effective advertising strategy.

- **Google Ads**:
  Google Ads, including Search Ads and Display Ads,

239

allows you to target people based on their search queries. For developers, this can be a great option if you're offering a service (e.g., consulting or tutoring) or if you want to advertise specific content (e.g., courses or blog posts).

- o **Example**: A web developer offering services might target keywords like "React developer for hire" or "custom WordPress developer" to appear in search results when someone looks for those services.

- **LinkedIn   Ads**:
  LinkedIn Ads are particularly effective for professional services, like consulting, as the platform is focused on business and career networking. LinkedIn allows you to target specific industries, job titles, company sizes, and geographic regions, making it easier to find clients who are looking for your services.

  - o **Example**: A developer specializing in cloud computing might use LinkedIn Ads to target CTOs of companies in need of cloud migration services.

- **Facebook/Instagram   Ads**:
  These platforms are great for creating brand

awareness and generating leads for more general offerings, like online courses, workshops, or webinars. They offer detailed targeting options based on interests, behaviors, and demographics.

- o **Example**: A developer offering an online course on web development might target people interested in programming, coding boot camps, or web design.

2. Set Clear Goals for Your Advertising Campaign

Before launching any paid ads, set clear objectives for what you hope to achieve. Whether it's generating leads, driving traffic to your website, or growing your social media following, having a specific goal will help you measure the success of your campaigns.

- **Tip**: Your goal should align with where you are in your business. For instance, if you're just starting out, focus on brand awareness and lead generation. If you already have an established brand, you can focus more on conversion-based goals, like sales or consultations.

3. Budgeting for Ads

One of the keys to successful paid advertising is budgeting effectively. You can start with a small budget to test your ads and gradually scale them based on performance.

- **Tip**: Start with low-budget campaigns and monitor their performance. Once you see what works, you can increase your budget for the best-performing ads.
- **Example**: You might start with $10 a day for a Google Ads campaign targeting specific keywords and use the data to optimize your campaign.

Setting Up Targeted Ads That Highlight Your Skills and Services

To make your ads work for you, they need to be targeted and tailored to your services. Here's how to set up your ads effectively:

1. Choose the Right Ad Type

Ads can be in the form of text ads, display ads, video ads, or sponsored posts, depending on the platform. The format you choose should match your goals and the audience you're targeting.

- **Google Ads**: For service-based businesses, Google Search Ads (text-based) work best as they appear when people search for services like yours. Display Ads are great for brand awareness as they visually showcase your skills or projects.

- **LinkedIn Ads**: Sponsored Content or InMail ads work well for consultants looking to target professionals in specific industries or job roles. These can be used to showcase case studies, blog posts, or even free resources like webinars.

2. Create Compelling Ad Copy

The ad copy should highlight your expertise and make a compelling case for why people should work with you. Focus on your unique value proposition (UVP) and include a call-to-action (CTA) to guide people toward the next step.

- **Tip**: Keep your copy concise, focused on benefits, and clear about what you're offering.

- **Example**: A freelance developer might write: "Need a React expert for your next project? Contact me for top-tier web applications. Book a free consultation today!"

3. Use Eye-Catching Visuals (For Display Ads and Social Media Ads)

If you're using display ads, video ads, or sponsored social media posts, make sure to use high-quality visuals that catch attention. Include screenshots of your projects, before-and-after comparisons, or videos demonstrating your expertise.

- **Tip**: Make sure your branding (logo, colors, etc.) is consistent across your ad visuals to reinforce your personal brand.
- **Example**: A developer who runs a blog about web development might use a vibrant banner ad that showcases a screenshot of a recent tutorial, with a CTA like "Learn How to Build a Portfolio Website - Click Here!"

4. Set Up Conversion Tracking

It's essential to track the performance of your ads to see which ones are delivering results. Conversion tracking allows you to see how many people clicked on your ad and took the desired action, whether it's signing up for a newsletter, booking a consultation, or purchasing a course.

- **Tip**: Set up goals in Google Analytics or use the tracking tools provided by the ad platform to measure conversions. This data will help you refine and optimize your ads over time.

- **Example**: You can track conversions on a landing page where clients book a consultation. If you're running a LinkedIn ad campaign for consulting, make sure you can track how many people book a session after clicking on the ad.

Case Studies of Developers Who Have Used Paid Ads Effectively

1. **Brad Traversy (Traversy Media)** Brad Traversy, a well-known web development educator, used paid advertising to promote his online courses and tutorials. He utilized Facebook and Google Ads to target aspiring web developers and boost the visibility of his tutorials on platforms like Udemy. By running highly targeted ad campaigns, Brad successfully grew his following and increased course sales.

    o **Key Takeaway**: Brad leveraged paid ads to reach his target audience—people interested in web development courses—focusing on

245

specific demographics such as aspiring developers or those interested in upgrading their skills.

2. **Mosh Hamedani (CodeWithMosh)** Mosh Hamedani, another influential software development educator, used paid ads to promote his online courses. Mosh ran targeted Facebook and Google Ads campaigns to promote his courses in full-stack JavaScript and React development. His ads targeted developers looking to level up their skills, and he used compelling video content to showcase the value of his courses.

   o **Key Takeaway**: Mosh's success shows the power of using paid ads to promote educational content. By targeting specific skills and creating engaging video ads, he was able to attract students interested in professional development.

3. **Kent C. Dodds (Epic React)** Kent C. Dodds, a React and JavaScript educator, utilized Facebook Ads and Google Ads to market his flagship course, "Epic React." He created highly targeted campaigns that focused on developers who were specifically looking to improve their React skills. His ads often featured

testimonials from satisfied students, as well as snippets from his course.

- o **Key Takeaway**: Kent's strategy to use ads with social proof (testimonials and reviews) helped create trust and persuaded developers to enroll in his course. His targeted ad campaigns on Facebook and Google helped him scale his brand.

4. **Chris Courses (ChrisCourses.com)** Chris, a developer and educator at ChrisCourses.com, used Google Ads and Instagram Ads to promote his web development tutorials and courses. He utilized targeted campaigns to reach people interested in web development and tech education, driving traffic to his website and YouTube channel. His paid ads included offers for free tutorials to capture leads.

- o **Key Takeaway**: Chris successfully used a combination of Google Ads and Instagram Ads to target young developers and those looking to learn specific web development skills. He used lead magnets (free tutorials) in his ads to build an email list, which he later used to promote paid courses.

Conclusion

Leveraging paid advertising is a powerful way to increase the visibility of your personal brand as a developer. Whether you're offering consulting services, promoting an online course, or looking to build a larger following, paid ads on platforms like Google, LinkedIn, Facebook, and Instagram can help you reach a highly targeted audience. By setting up targeted campaigns, creating compelling ad copy, and monitoring performance, you can effectively grow your brand and attract more opportunities.

In the next chapter, we will explore strategies for building long-term brand sustainability and ensuring continued success as a developer.

CHAPTER 22

MANAGING YOUR ONLINE REPUTATION

How to Monitor and Manage Your Online Reputation as a Developer

In today's digital age, your online reputation can significantly influence your career opportunities and professional relationships. Whether you are a freelancer, consultant, or full-time developer, your reputation can impact the trust potential clients, employers, and peers place in you. Managing your online presence is crucial for ensuring that the perception of you aligns with your personal brand. Here's how you can monitor and manage your online reputation effectively:

1. Google Yourself Regularly

One of the first steps in managing your online reputation is to monitor what others are saying about you. Regularly Google your name to see what comes up in search results. This gives you insight into how you are being perceived and allows you to track any mentions of your name on blogs, forums, social media, or news articles.

- **Tip**: Set up a Google Alert with your name to get notifications whenever your name appears in new search results or articles. This ensures you stay informed about any new content related to your personal brand.

2. Use Social Media Monitoring Tools

Tools like Mention, Brand24, or BuzzSumo allow you to track mentions of your name, projects, or business across social media platforms and websites. These tools provide real-time alerts so you can stay on top of discussions about you or your work.

- **Tip**: Set up alerts for keywords related to your niche or work, such as "React developer" or "Python tutorials." This will help you stay updated on trends, competitor activity, and discussions where you could potentially engage.

3. Be Active on Professional Platforms

Platforms like LinkedIn, GitHub, and StackOverflow are essential for developers looking to build and manage their professional reputation. By contributing valuable content, participating in discussions, and showcasing your skills, you build a positive online presence that positions you as an expert in your field.

- **Tip**: Regularly update your LinkedIn profile with new skills, projects, and accomplishments. Contribute answers to questions on StackOverflow to establish yourself as an expert in your area.

4. Control Your Own Website or Blog

Owning your own website or blog is one of the best ways to control your online reputation. This platform allows you to share your thoughts, showcase your work, and provide testimonials from satisfied clients or colleagues. A professional website serves as a central hub for everything related to your career and personal brand.

- **Tip**: Make sure your website is up-to-date with your portfolio, achievements, and contact information. Write blog posts that offer valuable insights into your

251

areas of expertise, which will help position you as a thought leader in your niche.

5. Engage with Your Audience and Community

Interacting with your audience and community helps you maintain a positive reputation and shows that you are approachable and professional. Respond to questions, share useful information, and engage with people who follow your work online.

- **Tip**: Be proactive in engaging with followers on platforms like Twitter, LinkedIn, or GitHub. Positive, meaningful interactions can help boost your reputation and foster a loyal community of supporters.

Tools and Strategies for Handling Negative Feedback or Criticism

No matter how well you manage your online presence, negative feedback or criticism is inevitable. How you handle it is what truly matters. Here are some tools and strategies to effectively manage negative feedback and maintain your reputation:

1. Respond Calmly and Professionally

When faced with criticism, it's important to remain calm and professional. Avoid responding impulsively or defensively. Take the time to understand the feedback and assess whether there is any truth to it. Acknowledging feedback gracefully and offering solutions when necessary can turn a negative situation into a positive one.

- **Tip**: Apologize if necessary, offer a constructive response, and provide a clear solution or next step. This shows that you are accountable and willing to improve.
- **Example**: If a client expresses dissatisfaction with your work, acknowledge their concerns and offer to make revisions or provide additional support. This demonstrates your professionalism and commitment to customer satisfaction.

2. Use Tools to Monitor Social Media Conversations

If you receive negative feedback or criticism on social media, it's important to track these conversations so you can respond promptly. Tools like Hootsuite, Sprout Social, or Social Mention allow you to monitor social media discussions, making it easier to address concerns before they escalate.

- **Tip**: Set up alerts for keywords related to your name or brand, and engage with negative posts as soon as possible. Responding quickly shows that you care about your reputation and are proactive in resolving issues.

3. Handle Trolls and Online Bullies Professionally

Unfortunately, trolls and online bullies may sometimes target you, especially if you have a large following. In these cases, it's important to avoid getting drawn into unnecessary arguments. Instead, stay professional, block or report abusive accounts, and move on.

- **Tip**: Don't feed the trolls. Responding to personal attacks often fuels the negativity. It's best to either ignore or report inappropriate comments and move forward with positive interactions.

4. Learn from Constructive Criticism

Not all criticism is negative. Constructive criticism can be a valuable tool for personal and professional growth. It helps you identify areas for improvement, refine your skills, and build better relationships with clients and peers.

- **Tip**: When you receive constructive feedback, take it seriously and use it to improve your future work. Acknowledging the feedback and making improvements shows maturity and dedication to your craft.

5. Know When to Take a Break

Sometimes, the best way to handle criticism or negativity is to step away from social media or online discussions for a short time. Taking a break can help you regain perspective, calm down, and come back with a fresh, rational approach to managing your reputation.

- **Tip**: Set boundaries for how much time you spend engaging online and avoid overreacting to every comment or piece of feedback.

Real-Life Examples of Developers Who Maintained a Strong Reputation Despite Challenges

1. **Joel Spolsky (Stack Overflow, Trello)** Joel Spolsky, the co-founder of Stack Overflow and Trello, has built a reputation as a thought leader in the tech community. Despite facing some criticism over the years—particularly around some decisions related to Stack Overflow—Joel has managed to maintain a strong personal brand by consistently providing valuable insights, responding to feedback, and owning his mistakes when necessary. His transparency and openness in handling criticism have only strengthened his reputation.

   o **Key Takeaway**: Joel's ability to accept criticism and use it to improve Stack Overflow and Trello shows that being open, transparent, and willing to adapt helps maintain a strong reputation even in the face of challenges.

2. **Sara Soueidan (Front-End Developer and Speaker)** Sara Soueidan, a well-known front-end developer and speaker, has built a strong online presence by consistently sharing her expertise on

CSS and front-end design. Although she has faced some online criticism for sharing controversial opinions, she has maintained her reputation by standing her ground, engaging constructively with her audience, and focusing on delivering high-quality content.

  o **Key Takeaway**: Sara's ability to handle criticism gracefully, while continuing to engage with her community in a professional manner, has allowed her to maintain a solid reputation in the front-end development space.

3. **Brad Frost (Atomic Design)** Brad Frost, the creator of Atomic Design, is widely respected for his work in the design systems field. He's faced occasional negative feedback, particularly regarding certain design philosophies, but his approach to handling these situations—by engaging respectfully and thoughtfully—has ensured that his reputation remains intact. Brad's focus on sharing his knowledge and collaborating with the community has helped him navigate challenges and maintain trust with his audience.

- o **Key Takeaway**: Brad's success comes from his consistent effort to share knowledge, maintain professionalism in the face of criticism, and his openness to learning and evolving in his field.

4. **Mosh Hamedani (CodeWithMosh)** Mosh Hamedani, a developer and educator with a successful online course business, has built a solid reputation through his work on Udemy and other platforms. Mosh has occasionally faced negative feedback, particularly from students regarding course pricing or specific teaching methods. However, Mosh responds to feedback, adjusts his courses based on constructive criticism, and offers refunds or clarifications where appropriate, ensuring his reputation remains strong.

- o **Key Takeaway**: Mosh's responsiveness to feedback and willingness to make adjustments to his content and services demonstrates that actively managing your reputation and addressing concerns can turn negative situations into opportunities for improvement.

Conclusion

Managing your online reputation as a developer is crucial for building trust, attracting clients, and maintaining professional relationships. By monitoring your online presence, responding to feedback in a constructive manner, and handling criticism professionally, you can ensure that your reputation remains strong. Engaging with your audience and focusing on continuous improvement will help you overcome challenges and build a lasting, positive brand in the tech community.

In the next chapter, we will explore how to scale your personal brand and turn your reputation into long-term success, opening new doors for career growth and business opportunities.

CHAPTER 23

PERSONAL BRAND CONSISTENCY

Why Consistency Across Platforms Is Key to a Successful Personal Brand

Consistency is one of the cornerstones of a successful personal brand. In the fast-paced world of technology and development, establishing a strong personal brand that resonates with your audience requires aligning your message, tone, and visual style across all platforms. When your brand is consistent, it builds recognition, trust, and credibility. Here's why consistency matters:

1. Builds Trust and Credibility

Consistency helps to build trust with your audience. When your messaging, visual style, and tone remain the same across different platforms, your audience knows what to expect from you. This reliability makes your brand feel more professional and trustworthy.

- **Example**: If a developer consistently shares high-quality content about React on LinkedIn, Twitter, and their blog, followers will begin to trust their advice and expertise in the React ecosystem.

2. Increases Brand Recognition

When you maintain consistency, your brand becomes recognizable. Whether it's your logo, your color scheme, or the tone of voice you use in your content, consistency helps create a cohesive identity that people can easily identify. Over time, this recognition can lead to more opportunities and a larger following.

- **Example**: A developer who uses the same color scheme, logo, and tagline on their website, LinkedIn, and social media accounts ensures that their brand is instantly recognizable, helping them stand out in a competitive space.

3. Reinforces Your Message

Consistent messaging ensures that your audience receives the same clear and concise information no matter where they find you. This reinforces the core values and expertise you want to communicate. Inconsistent messaging, on the other hand, can confuse potential clients or employers about who you are and what you offer.

- **Example**: If you are positioning yourself as an expert in web security, ensure that your content, such as blog posts, social media updates, and public speaking engagements, all convey that you are knowledgeable about this topic.

4. Creates a Professional Image

A consistent personal brand helps you come across as more professional and polished. When your profile pictures, website design, and tone align across platforms, it gives you a unified, well-thought-out image that makes a lasting impression on potential clients, employers, and collaborators.

- **Example**: A developer who maintains a professional LinkedIn profile, a polished website, and consistently shares insightful, relevant content on social media will be perceived as an expert in their field.

Tips for Maintaining Consistency in Your Message, Tone, and Style

Maintaining consistency in your personal brand requires intentional effort, attention to detail, and a clear strategy. Here are some tips to help you stay consistent across various platforms:

1. Define Your Brand's Core Values and Voice

- **Core Values**: Decide what your personal brand stands for. Are you focused on web development? Are you passionate about educating others? What makes you unique in your field? These core values should be communicated clearly in all your content, from your social media posts to your website bio.

- **Tone of Voice**: Establish a consistent tone for your communications. Your tone should match your brand's personality. Are you formal or informal? Inspirational or educational? Your tone should be consistent across all written and spoken communication.

    o **Tip**: If you're aiming for a professional tone, keep your messaging straightforward and clear. If your brand is more casual or approachable, your tone can be friendly and conversational.

- o **Example**: A developer who focuses on ethical hacking might maintain an authoritative and serious tone, while a developer specializing in JavaScript tutorials may adopt a more casual, friendly tone to make learning more accessible.

2. Use Consistent Visual Elements

- **Logo and Colors**: Ensure your logo, colors, and any visual elements stay consistent across all platforms. Your personal website, LinkedIn profile, GitHub, and any other platforms where you have a presence should feature the same design elements to reinforce your brand identity.
- **Profile and Banner Images**: Use the same professional headshot across your social media platforms and website. This creates a consistent visual identity and makes you easily recognizable.
- **Tip**: If you're not a designer, use tools like Canva to create simple but professional-looking visuals and templates for your profiles, blog posts, and social media content.

- **Example**: A developer's consistent use of the same logo and color palette across LinkedIn, GitHub, and their personal website helps reinforce their visual identity and makes them instantly recognizable to their audience.

3. Be Strategic with Content Themes

- **Content Focus**: Decide on specific themes or topics that you will consistently cover. These could include your expertise, current projects, industry news, or educational content. Stick to these topics so that your audience knows what to expect and recognizes your authority in that niche.
- **Content Calendar**: Plan your content ahead of time using a content calendar. This helps ensure that you're consistently sharing relevant content across platforms and keeping your message aligned.
- **Example**: If you're a developer specializing in cloud computing, make sure that the majority of your content—whether blog posts, videos, or social media updates—relates to this niche.

4. Repurpose Content for Different Platforms

- Repurposing your content for different platforms is an excellent way to maintain consistency while ensuring that each platform receives tailored content. For example, a blog post can be broken down into smaller, digestible social media posts or used to create a video or podcast episode.

- **Tip**: Don't simply copy-paste content across platforms; instead, tailor the content to fit the platform's style. A LinkedIn article may be more formal, while an Instagram post can be more casual and visual.

- **Example**: A blog post on "Best Practices for Building Secure APIs" can be repurposed into a LinkedIn article, a Twitter thread, and an Instagram infographic to maintain a consistent message across channels.

5. Engage Consistently with Your Audience

- **Respond to Comments and Messages**: Engaging with your audience shows that you are approachable and genuinely interested in their feedback. Regularly respond to comments, messages, and questions to build a stronger connection with your community.

- **Consistency in Posting**: Develop a regular posting schedule and stick to it. Whether you're posting once a week, bi-weekly, or monthly, maintaining a consistent rhythm helps you stay relevant in the minds of your audience.

- **Example**: If you're writing tutorials or sharing insights on LinkedIn, maintain a regular posting schedule to keep your audience engaged. Similarly, if you are an active member of developer forums or Slack groups, contribute consistently to stay visible.

Case Studies of Developers Who Have Built Consistent and Strong Brands

1. **Brad Traversy (Traversy Media)** Brad Traversy, a well-known educator in the web development space, has built a strong personal brand through consistency. He maintains a uniform approach to his brand across platforms, including his YouTube channel, blog, and social media. His focus on web development tutorials, personal projects, and

educational content has created a recognizable identity.

- o **Key Takeaway**: Brad's consistency in content focus, tone, and visual elements across his website, YouTube channel, and social media accounts has made him a go-to resource for aspiring developers, establishing a loyal following.

2. **Mosh Hamedani (CodeWithMosh)** Mosh Hamedani has become a trusted name in the tech education space by building a strong, consistent brand across all platforms. From his YouTube tutorials to his courses on Udemy, his branding (from his logo to his tone) remains consistent. His brand message—offering high-quality, easy-to-understand coding tutorials—has helped him attract a large, engaged audience.

- o **Key Takeaway**: Mosh's success lies in his ability to deliver a consistent message and educational experience across all content types, from video tutorials to written materials.

3. **Sarah Drasner (Vue.js, Web Animation Expert)** Sarah Drasner, an expert in web animations and

Vue.js, has built a strong brand through consistency in her content and public speaking. Whether it's her talks at conferences, her tutorials, or her personal blog, Sarah has maintained a consistent voice that focuses on educating the web development community. She also leverages her personal story to connect with her audience, reinforcing her professional identity.

o **Key Takeaway**: Sarah's consistent messaging, strong visual identity, and authoritative voice in the front-end development and animation spaces have helped her build a highly respected personal brand.

4. **Kent C. Dodds (Epic React)** Kent C. Dodds is known for his focus on React and JavaScript education. His brand is built on the consistent delivery of valuable, in-depth content. Kent maintains consistency through his blog, courses, and social media presence. His clear, approachable tone and focus on high-quality tutorials have made him one of the leading voices in the React community.

o **Key Takeaway**: Kent's ability to create content that is aligned with his brand values, from tutorials to conference talks, has made him a trusted resource for developers looking to master React.

Conclusion

Consistency is critical to building a strong personal brand as a developer. By aligning your message, tone, and style across platforms, you create a cohesive and recognizable identity that resonates with your audience. Consistent content creation, engagement, and visual elements help reinforce your professional image, leading to greater trust, recognition, and opportunities. The success stories of developers like Brad Traversy, Mosh Hamedani, and Sarah Drasner demonstrate that when your brand is consistent and aligned with your values, it can lead to long-term growth and a strong reputation in the industry.

In the next chapter, we will explore strategies for scaling your personal brand and turning your reputation into sustainable, long-term success.

CHAPTER 24

BECOMING A THOUGHT LEADER

What It Means to Be a Thought Leader in the Developer Community

A thought leader is someone recognized as an authority in their field, someone who inspires others with innovative ideas, and someone who shapes conversations within a specific community or industry. In the developer community, being a thought leader involves more than just having technical expertise; it's about influencing how others think, work, and evolve in their field. Here's what it means to be a thought leader in the developer community:

1. Sharing Insights and Innovative Ideas

A thought leader brings fresh perspectives to the table. They are constantly exploring new trends, technologies, and methodologies in the tech world and are unafraid to challenge the status quo. By sharing their insights, they spark discussions and help push the boundaries of what's possible in the field.

- **Example**: A developer who writes a blog post or speaks at a conference about a new JavaScript framework can influence others by shedding light on new tools that could potentially revolutionize web development.

2. Guiding and Mentoring Others

Thought leaders often take on the role of mentors, guiding others in their professional development. They share their experiences, offer advice, and provide solutions to common challenges. By helping others grow and learn, they contribute to the overall advancement of the developer community.

- **Example**: A senior developer who mentors junior developers, sharing best practices and career advice, can create a lasting impact on the next generation of tech talent.

3. Building a Strong Personal Brand

Thought leadership is tied to your personal brand. By consistently sharing valuable, actionable content, speaking at conferences, and engaging with your audience, you build your reputation as an expert in your niche. Thought leaders are known for their contributions and their ability to communicate complex ideas in an accessible and impactful way.

- **Example**: A developer with a strong presence on platforms like GitHub, LinkedIn, Twitter, and personal blogs becomes known for their expertise in specific technologies, frameworks, or methodologies.

4. Being Open to New Ideas and Continuous Learning

True thought leadership involves a willingness to adapt and evolve. As technology and trends shift, thought leaders stay ahead of the curve by continuously learning and adopting new practices. They are not just experts in their current domain; they are also future-focused, always looking for new ways to innovate and grow.

- **Example**: A developer who embraces new concepts, such as serverless computing or machine learning, and integrates them into their work shows a forward-thinking mindset that positions them as a leader.

How to Share Your Knowledge in Ways That Inspire and Lead Others

To become a thought leader, it's essential to share your knowledge in ways that inspire and lead others in the developer community. Here's how to do that effectively:

1. Create High-Quality, Educational Content

One of the most effective ways to share your knowledge is through high-quality content. Writing blog posts, creating tutorials, or recording video lessons on platforms like YouTube or Udemy allows you to communicate your ideas and expertise to a broad audience.

- **Tip**: Focus on creating content that addresses the specific challenges developers face. This could be in the form of tutorials, problem-solving guides, or insights into emerging trends.
- **Example**: A developer creating a tutorial on building scalable APIs with Node.js can provide practical, actionable insights that help others improve their coding practices.

2. Speak at Conferences and Meetups

Speaking at conferences, webinars, or meetups is one of the best ways to showcase your expertise and inspire others. By sharing your knowledge on a larger stage, you can influence not just your immediate audience but the broader developer community.

- **Tip**: Prepare talks that focus on both your technical knowledge and your experiences. Sharing personal stories about challenges you've faced and how you overcame them can make your presentations more relatable and impactful.
- **Example**: A developer speaking at a ReactJS conference about their journey of contributing to the React ecosystem and lessons learned along the way can inspire others to contribute to open-source projects.

3. Participate in Open Source and Developer Communities

Contributing to open-source projects is a powerful way to demonstrate thought leadership. By participating in or leading open-source initiatives, you are actively shaping the tools and frameworks that others in the community use, which can greatly enhance your reputation as a leader.

- **Tip**: Engage in developer communities, such as Stack Overflow, GitHub, or Reddit, where you can offer your expertise, provide feedback on code, and guide others through problem-solving processes.
- **Example**: A developer contributing to an open-source library and providing detailed documentation, tutorials, or user support is recognized as a thought leader in that specific field or framework.

4. Be a Mentor and Share Your Experience

Mentorship is a key part of being a thought leader. By helping others grow and advance in their careers, you not only pass on your knowledge but also inspire the next generation of developers. This can include offering advice, reviewing code, or simply sharing career insights with newcomers.

- **Tip**: Offer mentorship opportunities through platforms like LinkedIn, Slack communities, or online coding boot camps. You can also create a mentoring program or a developer group to foster knowledge-sharing and collaboration.

- **Example**: A senior developer who mentors junior developers by reviewing their code, providing career guidance, and offering constructive feedback is seen as a leader who is helping shape the future of the industry.

5. Write a Book or eBook

Writing a book or eBook about your area of expertise is a great way to solidify your position as a thought leader. A book not only allows you to share in-depth knowledge but also establishes you as an authority in your field.

- **Tip**: Focus on a niche topic that aligns with your expertise and passion. Provide practical advice, case studies, and real-world examples that offer tangible value to your readers.
- **Example**: A developer writing a book on "Building Scalable Web Applications with React and Node.js" provides an in-depth resource for developers looking to deepen their knowledge in full-stack development.

Stories of Developers Who Became Thought Leaders and Influencers

1. **Brad Traversy (Traversy Media)** Brad Traversy, a well-known web developer and educator, became a thought leader by consistently producing high-quality content on web development. He built a strong personal brand through his YouTube channel, Traversy Media, where he shares tutorials on everything from front-end technologies like React to back-end development with Node.js. Brad's consistent, high-value content has made him a trusted voice in the web development community.

    o   **Key Takeaway**: Brad's success as a thought leader comes from his commitment to educating the community and his willingness to share his journey, challenges, and solutions in an approachable way.

2. **Kent C. Dodds (Epic React)** Kent C. Dodds is a well-respected figure in the React ecosystem. He became a thought leader by creating educational resources, such as his "Epic React" course, and by regularly contributing to the developer community. Kent has written blog posts, participated in talks, and

created valuable content that helps developers master React.

- o **Key Takeaway**: Kent's focus on sharing high-quality educational content, combined with his clear and engaging teaching style, has positioned him as a thought leader in the React and JavaScript communities.

3. **Mosh Hamedani (CodeWithMosh)** Mosh Hamedani is another example of a developer who became a thought leader by creating high-quality educational content. He built his personal brand by offering premium courses on full-stack JavaScript, React, and Python, and he gained credibility through his consistent approach to teaching.

- o **Key Takeaway**: Mosh's ability to break down complex concepts into easy-to-understand lessons has made him a go-to educator for developers looking to improve their skills. His transition from YouTube tutorials to full-fledged courses demonstrates how thought leadership can be scaled.

4. **Sarah Drasner (Vue.js, Web Animation Expert)** Sarah Drasner is a front-end development expert, particularly in Vue.js and web animations. Sarah

became a thought leader through her speaking engagements, contributions to Vue.js, and educational content on topics like SVG animations. She also shares her expertise in the community through blog posts, tutorials, and talks at conferences.

- o **Key Takeaway**: Sarah's journey to thought leadership was built on her passion for creating beautiful web experiences, her contributions to the open-source community, and her ability to communicate complex ideas in an accessible manner.

Conclusion

Becoming a thought leader in the developer community is about more than just technical expertise. It's about sharing your knowledge, inspiring others, and helping shape the future of technology. By consistently creating valuable content, mentoring others, participating in open-source projects, and positioning yourself as an expert, you can build a strong, influential personal brand. Developers like Brad Traversy, Kent C. Dodds, and Sarah Drasner have successfully done this by focusing on education, building relationships, and consistently offering value to the community.

In the next chapter, we will explore strategies for sustaining your thought leadership and continuing to expand your influence in the tech industry.

CHAPTER 25

SCALING YOUR PERSONAL BRAND

How to Take Your Personal Brand from Local to Global Recognition

Scaling your personal brand from local recognition to global prominence is a process that requires strategic planning, consistent effort, and leveraging both your existing network and new opportunities. It's not just about growing your audience; it's about positioning yourself as a recognized authority in your field on an international scale. Here's how you can scale your personal brand:

1. Focus on Creating High-Quality, Shareable Content

The content you produce is the cornerstone of your brand. To scale your personal brand globally, you need to create content that resonates with a broad audience and is easily shareable. This includes blog posts, video tutorials, courses, and public talks that highlight your expertise in your niche.

- **Tip**: Focus on creating evergreen content that provides lasting value, such as tutorials, guides, or thought-provoking articles that will continue to attract attention over time.

- **Example**: A developer who creates in-depth, highly-shareable tutorials on platforms like YouTube or Medium can gain global recognition by appealing to a diverse audience. People across the world search for tutorials on specific technologies, and if your content ranks well on search engines, it can spread rapidly.

2. Leverage SEO (Search Engine Optimization)

Optimizing your content for search engines is crucial for scaling your brand globally. By targeting keywords that are highly relevant to your niche and crafting high-quality content that answers the questions people are searching for, you can increase your visibility on Google and other search engines.

- **Tip**: Use tools like Google Keyword Planner or Ahrefs to research keywords that your target audience is searching for. Create content around these keywords and ensure that your website or blog is optimized for SEO.

- **Example**: A developer who writes blog posts on "How to Use React Hooks" or "Best Practices for Node.js" can rank well for those keywords, attracting a global audience interested in learning those technologies.

3. Participate in International Communities

One of the most effective ways to scale your brand is by engaging with international developer communities. This could be through forums, GitHub, Stack Overflow, Reddit, and social media platforms like Twitter and LinkedIn. By contributing to discussions, answering questions, and sharing your expertise, you can increase your visibility across the globe.

- **Tip**: Join international developer forums, contribute to open-source projects, and engage with global communities. Offer solutions to problems that developers worldwide are facing.
- **Example**: A developer who frequently contributes to international open-source projects like Vue.js or Node.js can gain recognition globally. These

contributions will not only enhance your brand but also position you as an influential member of the global developer community.

4. Speak at International Conferences and Meetups

Public speaking is one of the fastest ways to scale your personal brand globally. By speaking at international conferences, webinars, or developer meetups, you can share your expertise with a wider audience and build a reputation as a thought leader in your niche.

- **Tip**: Start by speaking at local or regional events and gradually move to international conferences. Many tech conferences also offer virtual options, which make it easier for you to speak to a global audience without leaving home.
- **Example**: A developer who speaks at global conferences like Google I/O, ReactConf, or JSConf can reach thousands of attendees and build a global following. The exposure from such events often leads to new career opportunities, collaborations, and partnerships.

Expanding Your Brand with Advanced Techniques and Partnerships

Once you've established a strong local presence, it's time to scale your brand with more advanced techniques and strategic partnerships. Here are some ways to expand your brand further:

1. Collaborate with Other Industry Leaders

Partnering with other established developers, influencers, or brands can help you expand your reach and credibility. Collaboration can take many forms, from co-hosting webinars and workshops to contributing to joint projects or writing guest blog posts.

- **Tip**: Identify potential partners who share similar values and audiences, but bring unique strengths or expertise to the table. This will allow both parties to benefit from each other's networks and experiences.
- **Example**: A developer specializing in front-end technologies could collaborate with a back-end expert to co-host a webinar series on full-stack development, combining both audiences for greater reach.

2. Launch a Product or Service

Launching your own product, such as a premium online course, eBook, or even a SaaS tool, can help expand your personal brand by creating a tangible offering that people can purchase or use. This not only provides you with a new revenue stream but also solidifies your position as a leader in your field.

- **Tip**: Before launching a product, build an email list or social media following so you have an audience ready to support your launch. Focus on creating high-quality products that meet the needs of your target audience.
- **Example**: A developer who creates a premium online course on "Mastering React" or "Building Scalable Node.js Applications" can position themselves as an authority in their niche while monetizing their expertise.

3. Get Featured in Media or Industry Publications

Getting featured in respected publications, podcasts, or media outlets can massively increase your global recognition. Being quoted in well-known tech blogs, interviews, or podcasts positions you as an authority figure and gives your brand exposure to new audiences.

- **Tip**: Reach out to editors or podcast hosts with a pitch highlighting your expertise and why your insights would be valuable to their audience. Offer to share case studies, industry predictions, or actionable tips in an interview.
- **Example**: A developer who is regularly featured on platforms like Smashing Magazine or Medium, or who appears as a guest on tech podcasts like The Changelog or React Podcast, can build significant credibility and global visibility.

4. Invest in Paid Advertising

Running paid ads on platforms like LinkedIn, Google, or Facebook can help scale your brand globally by reaching highly-targeted audiences. While organic growth is essential, paid ads provide a way to accelerate your reach and connect with potential clients or followers worldwide.

- **Tip**: Start with a small budget and test various ads to see which ones perform best. Focus on targeting the right audience using demographics, interests, and location-based targeting.

- **Example**: A developer offering consulting services might run a targeted LinkedIn ad campaign aimed at CTOs or startups in need of web development services, allowing them to expand their reach and attract international clients.

Real-World Examples of Developers Who Scaled Their Personal Brand to New Heights

1. **Brad Traversy (Traversy Media)** Brad Traversy built a global brand by consistently providing high-quality web development tutorials on his YouTube channel, Traversy Media. He also created premium courses on platforms like Udemy, which brought him recognition not only locally but also internationally. Brad's brand grew through strategic use of YouTube, blog posts, collaborations with other developers, and the release of highly-valued paid content.

    o **Key Takeaway**: Brad leveraged content creation, online courses, and collaborations to scale his brand globally. His consistency, educational focus, and engagement with the developer community have made him a trusted name worldwide.

2. **Mosh Hamedani (CodeWithMosh)** Mosh Hamedani transitioned from being a local educator to a global thought leader by focusing on creating in-depth video courses, offering valuable free content on YouTube, and building a premium online course platform. His ability to communicate complex topics in an accessible manner allowed him to attract a global audience and grow his brand into a recognized business.

   o **Key Takeaway**: Mosh's strategic use of online courses, YouTube tutorials, and a strong personal brand helped him scale his influence globally. By focusing on value-driven content, he built an international community of learners and customers.

3. **Kent C. Dodds (Epic React)** Kent C. Dodds is a renowned React educator who built his global brand by creating one of the most successful React courses, "Epic React." He combined his technical expertise with a focus on clear, actionable teaching, and his brand grew as a result. Kent's contributions to open-source, his engaging blog, and his strong presence at

international conferences helped him gain recognition globally.

- o **Key Takeaway**: Kent's focus on high-quality, specialized educational content and his contributions to the React community allowed him to scale his personal brand globally. His online courses, blog, and conference talks have made him a well-known figure in the JavaScript community.

4. **Sara Drasner (Vue.js and Web Animation Expert)** Sara Drasner, a front-end developer and expert in web animations, scaled her personal brand globally through her contributions to Vue.js, her speaking engagements at international conferences, and her educational content. By sharing her deep knowledge of web animations, Sara became a leading voice in the developer community and gained a global following.

   - o **Key Takeaway**: Sara scaled her personal brand by consistently sharing her knowledge on international platforms and engaging with a global audience. Her focus on education, public speaking, and contributions to Vue.js helped her build a strong, global personal brand.

Conclusion

Scaling your personal brand from local recognition to global prominence requires a combination of strategic content creation, networking, collaborations, and utilizing advanced techniques like SEO, public speaking, and paid advertising. By building a consistent and value-driven presence across various platforms, engaging with international communities, and offering educational resources or services, you can extend your influence far beyond your immediate network.

In the next chapter, we will explore how to sustain and evolve your personal brand for long-term success and ensure that it continues to grow with the changing tech landscape.

CHAPTER 26

OVERCOMING CHALLENGES IN PERSONAL BRANDING

Common Challenges Developers Face While Building Their Personal Brands

Building a personal brand as a developer can be a rewarding endeavor, but it's not without its challenges. Many developers face obstacles that can slow their progress or even cause them to doubt themselves. Below are some of the common challenges developers face while building their personal brands:

1. Overwhelm from Content Creation

Developing and maintaining a consistent stream of content—whether it's blog posts, social media updates, or videos—can be overwhelming. Developers often struggle to find the time to create content while juggling their regular work, personal projects, and other responsibilities.

- **Solution**: Start small by creating a content calendar and focusing on creating one piece of content per week. Repurpose content across multiple platforms (e.g., turn a blog post into a video or social media posts) to reduce the workload.

2. Limited Exposure and Visibility

As a developer, it can be hard to stand out in a saturated market. There are many talented developers, so it can be difficult to get noticed, especially when just starting out.

- **Solution**: Focus on niches that you are passionate about and become known for your expertise in those areas. Engage actively with developer communities and contribute to open-source projects to gain recognition.

3. Self-Doubt and Imposter Syndrome

Imposter syndrome is a feeling of inadequacy or self-doubt despite evident success or expertise. Many developers feel that they aren't "qualified enough" to share their knowledge or that they aren't experts compared to others in the field.

- **Solution**: Remind yourself that everyone has something unique to offer. Focus on the value you can bring to others rather than comparing yourself to others. Start small by sharing what you know, and remember that even sharing the basics can be helpful to others.

4. Fear of Failure

The fear of failure can paralyze developers from taking the necessary steps to build their personal brand. The thought of putting yourself out there and facing criticism or rejection can be daunting.

- **Solution**: Embrace failure as part of the learning process. Accept that not everything will be perfect, and that's okay. Start by taking small risks—perhaps publishing your first blog post or giving a small talk—and gradually work your way up. With time, you'll grow more comfortable with the process.

5. Burnout from Overcommitment

Building a personal brand requires consistent effort, but overworking yourself can lead to burnout. Trying to do too much too quickly—such as posting daily or taking on too many side projects—can lead to exhaustion and a lack of motivation.

- **Solution**: Pace yourself and set realistic goals. Create a sustainable schedule that allows for personal time and recovery. Focus on long-term growth rather than instant success.

How to Overcome Imposter Syndrome, Fear of Failure, and Burnout

While challenges like imposter syndrome, fear of failure, and burnout are common, they don't have to stop you from building a successful personal brand. Here's how to overcome these obstacles:

1. Overcoming Imposter Syndrome

Imposter syndrome can hold you back from sharing your expertise with the world. However, it's essential to recognize that everyone starts somewhere, and even if you're not the "most advanced" in your field, you still have valuable knowledge to share.

- **Tip**: Focus on the progress you've made, not just your perceived lack of knowledge. Start by creating beginner-friendly content that others can relate to and gradually build up to more advanced topics as you grow.

- **Reframe Your Mindset**: Remind yourself that being a "beginner" or "intermediate" developer is still valuable to others who are just starting their learning journey.

- **Example**: A developer with limited experience in a particular framework may feel insecure about teaching it. However, by sharing their journey of learning the framework, they can help others who are in the same position. Over time, as they gain more expertise, their content can evolve.

2. Conquering Fear of Failure

Fear of failure is something everyone faces, especially when stepping into new territory. It can manifest as the fear of putting out content, speaking publicly, or launching a new product. But the key is to reframe failure not as something to be feared but as an opportunity for growth.

- **Tip**: Break down big goals into smaller, manageable steps. Start with small, low-risk projects that you can improve upon over time. For example, if you're afraid of public speaking, start by speaking to small groups or hosting webinars before applying to larger conferences.

- **Embrace a Growth Mindset**: Recognize that failure is an essential part of success. Each failure teaches you something valuable that will bring you closer to your next achievement.

- **Example**: A developer who is launching their first online course may worry about its success. Instead of fearing failure, they can focus on creating the best content possible and consider any mistakes or critiques as opportunities to improve for the next version of the course.

3. Avoiding Burnout

Burnout is a significant challenge for developers trying to balance building their brand with their work and personal lives. It can be difficult to keep up the energy required for consistent content creation while maintaining a healthy work-life balance.

- **Tip**: Take regular breaks and time off to recharge. Set boundaries on how much time you will spend on personal branding activities. It's important to schedule downtime for relaxation, hobbies, and spending time with family and friends.

- **Focus on Quality, Not Quantity**: Instead of trying to post or create content every day, aim for high-quality content that can make a real impact. Slow and steady progress is often more sustainable than pushing yourself to do everything at once.

- **Example**: A developer who feels overwhelmed by the pressure to post daily might decide to scale back and focus on posting once a week. This allows for more thoughtful, higher-quality content and prevents them from feeling burnt out.

Stories of Developers Who Pushed Through Obstacles to Build Their Personal Brand

1. **Brad Traversy (Traversy Media)** Brad Traversy, a well-known web developer and educator, faced many challenges early in his career, including a lack of exposure and self-doubt. However, he pushed through by consistently creating valuable content on YouTube and other platforms. Brad's determination to keep improving his tutorials and provide real-

world coding advice helped him build a strong personal brand.

- o **Key Takeaway**: Brad's persistence despite early challenges shows that consistency and the willingness to learn from failures can pay off in the long run. He didn't let imposter syndrome or fear of failure stop him from teaching others.

2. **Mosh Hamedani (CodeWithMosh)** Mosh Hamedani had to overcome the challenge of imposter syndrome when he first started sharing his knowledge online. Coming from a software engineering background, he initially doubted his ability to teach others. However, by focusing on creating high-quality tutorials and courses, he was able to build a global following and establish himself as an authority in the field of software development.

- o **Key Takeaway**: Mosh's journey demonstrates that focusing on providing value, even when you feel like you're not "good enough," can lead to great success. He overcame his self-doubt by staying committed to his goal of educating others.

3. **Kent C. Dodds (Epic React)** Kent C. Dodds, a renowned React educator, faced challenges in building his personal brand, particularly around imposter syndrome. However, he pushed through by focusing on his passion for teaching and sharing what he knew. Through his blog, courses, and contributions to open-source, Kent built a strong reputation in the React community, proving that sharing your journey and knowledge can resonate with others.

   o **Key Takeaway**: Kent's story shows that personal branding is about sharing your knowledge and experience, even if you're not at the "top" of your field. By focusing on helping others learn and grow, you can carve out a niche for yourself.

4. **Sarah Drasner (Vue.js, Web Animation Expert)** Sarah Drasner, a prominent figure in the Vue.js community and an expert in web animations, initially faced challenges in scaling her personal brand. Despite these obstacles, she overcame self-doubt by contributing to open-source projects and speaking at conferences. Through persistence and dedication,

Sarah became a thought leader in the front-end development community.

- **Key Takeaway**: Sarah's journey demonstrates the importance of embracing new opportunities, like open-source contributions and public speaking, to overcome challenges and build a personal brand in the tech industry.

Conclusion

Overcoming the challenges of building a personal brand is an inevitable part of the process. Whether it's imposter syndrome, fear of failure, or burnout, these obstacles can feel overwhelming, but they don't have to hold you back. By maintaining a growth mindset, setting realistic goals, and being consistent, you can push through these challenges and continue to build a strong personal brand. Developers like Brad Traversy, Mosh Hamedani, Kent C. Dodds, and Sarah Drasner have shown that persistence, hard work, and the willingness to learn from setbacks can help you achieve long-term success.

In the next chapter, we will explore how to sustain your personal brand over the long term, ensuring that it continues to evolve and grow with your career.

CHAPTER 27

THE FUTURE OF YOUR PERSONAL BRAND

How to Continue Growing and Evolving Your Personal Brand Over Time

Building a personal brand is an ongoing journey, and to stay relevant in the fast-paced tech industry, it's crucial to continue growing and evolving your brand. As your skills and career progress, so should your brand. Here's how you can keep evolving and scaling your personal brand over time:

1. Keep Learning and Adapting

The tech industry is ever-evolving, with new tools, languages, and frameworks emerging regularly. To maintain your relevance, commit to lifelong learning. Stay current with industry trends, and continually expand your expertise by exploring new technologies, attending conferences, and taking courses.

- **Tip**: Regularly refresh your skills by pursuing certifications, learning new programming languages, or staying updated with new development practices. This ensures you remain an expert in your field.

- **Example**: A web developer who started out with JavaScript may expand their brand to include knowledge of emerging technologies like WebAssembly or Progressive Web Apps (PWAs), ensuring they remain at the cutting edge of web development.

2. Diversify Your Content

As you grow in your career and expertise, diversifying the type of content you produce will help reach broader audiences. If you've been focusing primarily on written content, consider adding videos, podcasts, or webinars. Diversifying your content delivery allows you to reach different types of learners and establishes your brand across multiple channels.

- **Tip**: Experiment with new formats such as YouTube videos, live coding sessions, online workshops, or podcast guest appearances. By doing so, you can reach new audiences who might prefer a different content format.

- **Example**: A developer who's been blogging for years might start recording video tutorials or hosting live coding sessions on platforms like Twitch, expanding their brand's presence across new media.

3. Continuously Engage with Your Audience

Engagement is key to maintaining a strong personal brand. As your audience grows, it's important to stay connected with them. Regularly respond to comments, share personal insights, and keep the conversation going on platforms like Twitter, LinkedIn, and GitHub. Building a community around your brand ensures that your audience stays loyal and engaged over time.

- **Tip**: Schedule time to engage with your followers regularly, respond to their questions, and offer helpful advice. Share updates about your own learning journey and accomplishments to inspire your audience.
- **Example**: A developer who regularly interacts with their community on Stack Overflow or Twitter, answering questions, providing solutions, and

engaging in discussions, helps maintain a loyal following.

4. Evolve Your Message

As you progress in your career, your expertise and focus may shift. It's important that your brand evolves with you. Periodically reevaluate your message to ensure it reflects your current expertise, values, and passions. This keeps your brand authentic and aligned with where you are in your career.

- **Tip**: Reassess your brand's mission and message every year to ensure it reflects your growth and aligns with your long-term career goals. If you shift your focus to new areas, update your content to match your new expertise.
- **Example**: A developer who started their brand focused on front-end development may evolve their message to include full-stack development or DevOps as they gain new skills and experience.

The Importance of Staying Adaptable in an Ever-Changing Tech Landscape

The technology industry is notorious for its rapid pace of change. What's popular today may be obsolete in a few years. To maintain a successful personal brand, it's essential to stay adaptable and open to new opportunities. Here's why adaptability is crucial:

1. Embrace Emerging Technologies

Technologies evolve, and new tools are constantly emerging. The key to staying relevant is to remain open to learning and adopting these new technologies. Being an early adopter of emerging trends can position you as a thought leader in new areas of tech.

- **Tip**: Experiment with new technologies and tools in your personal projects. Write about them, share your experiences, and educate others about how they work.
- **Example**: A developer who embraces the rise of AI, machine learning, or blockchain technology early on can become a go-to expert in those fields and attract new opportunities.

2. Pivot When Necessary

The market and industry demands change. If you're passionate about something but see diminishing returns or interest, it's important to pivot and refocus. For example, if your brand revolves around a specific technology that's becoming obsolete, take steps to transition your brand to reflect newer, in-demand technologies.

- **Tip**: Regularly analyze industry trends to assess the future outlook of your niche. If necessary, pivot to a new area that excites you and offers more opportunities for growth.
- **Example**: A developer who started with a focus on Flash development but transitioned to learning modern web standards such as HTML5 and JavaScript frameworks like React when the market shifted.

3. Adapt to New Platforms and Opportunities

As new platforms emerge, it's essential to consider whether they offer opportunities for expanding your brand. Social media platforms and tools change over time—what works on Twitter today may not work tomorrow, and platforms like

TikTok or Clubhouse may offer new ways to reach your audience.

- **Tip**: Stay aware of new platforms and assess whether they align with your goals. If a platform is gaining popularity within your niche, consider how you can use it to further promote your brand.
- **Example**: A developer who quickly embraced platforms like TikTok or Clubhouse, which were once new and emerging, could build an entirely new audience by creating content specifically designed for those formats.

Long-Term Strategies for Maintaining Your Personal Brand and Staying Relevant

Building a personal brand is not a one-time effort but a long-term strategy. To sustain and maintain your personal brand over the years, focus on the following strategies:

1. Build Strategic Partnerships

As your personal brand grows, you will have the opportunity to collaborate with other professionals and brands. Strategic partnerships can open doors to new audiences, provide fresh content opportunities, and increase your visibility.

- **Tip**: Seek out partnerships with other thought leaders, tech companies, or influencers in your niche. Whether it's through joint ventures, podcast collaborations, or co-hosted events, partnerships can help you expand your reach.
- **Example**: A developer partnering with a tech company to offer exclusive tutorials on their platform could tap into the company's established audience, creating a win-win situation for both parties.

2. Continue Creating High-Quality, Evergreen Content

High-quality content is what builds your brand in the long term. Make sure the content you produce is valuable, timeless, and optimized for long-term engagement. This could include writing detailed technical guides, creating tutorial series, or developing an educational course that can be used by people for years.

- **Tip**: Focus on creating content that solves common problems, provides in-depth explanations, or tackles niche topics that will remain relevant to your audience over time.

- **Example**: A developer creating a well-researched and in-depth course on a popular framework will continue to attract new learners for years as the course remains a valuable resource.

3. Stay Authentic

Authenticity is key to maintaining a strong and relatable brand. As your career progresses, remember to stay true to your values and passions. Your authenticity resonates with your audience and helps build deeper, more meaningful connections.

- **Tip**: Be transparent about your journey, the mistakes you've made, and the lessons you've learned along the way. Sharing your personal story will help others relate to you and stay engaged with your brand.
- **Example**: A developer who shares not only their successes but also their challenges and failures can build a genuine connection with their audience, making their personal brand more relatable and trustworthy.

4. Measure and Analyze Your Brand's Performance

Regularly analyze the performance of your personal brand. Use analytics tools to measure the effectiveness of your content, engagement, and overall brand growth. Identify which strategies work best and refine your approach based on data.

- **Tip**: Set clear, measurable goals for your personal brand. Regularly track metrics such as website traffic, social media engagement, course enrollments, or consulting inquiries to ensure that your brand is growing in the right direction.
- **Example**: A developer tracking the success of their blog posts, YouTube videos, or courses can use data to tweak their content strategy and optimize future growth.

Conclusion

The future of your personal brand depends on your ability to stay adaptable, evolve your message, and keep up with the ever-changing tech landscape. By continuing to learn, diversify your content, engage with your community, and embrace new opportunities, you can ensure that your personal brand remains relevant for years to come. Long-term strategies like building partnerships, staying authentic, and consistently creating high-quality content will help you maintain and expand your influence in the developer community.

As you continue to scale your personal brand, remember that the journey is ongoing. With dedication, perseverance, and a focus on value, you can sustain a successful and impactful personal brand that adapts to the future of tech.

www.ingramcontent.com/pod-product-compliance
Lightning Source LLC
LaVergne TN
LVHW051432050326
832903LV00030BD/3048